HOW TO MAKE IT IN THE TRAVEL INDUSTRY

HOW TO MAKE IT IN THE TRAVEL INDUSTRY

JOANNA GRIGG

Virgin

First published in Great Britain in 2001 by
Virgin Publishing Ltd
Thames Wharf Studios
Rainville Road
London W6 9HA

A catalogue record for the book is available from
the British Library.

ISBN 0 7535 0419 7

Designed and typeset by Roger Kohn Designs
Printed and bound in Great Britain by
Mackays of Chatham

ABOUT THE AUTHOR

Joanna Grigg writes anything and everything and with her background in careers and recruitment, careers guides are what she does best. She worked in sales, accountancy and mothering before settling down to her current mix of working for a careers service, teaching writing skills and personal and career development, and writing books on interesting topics. Of this book she says: 'If I had to chuck it all in and do something else I would join the travel biz'. So perhaps that's next.

ACKNOWLEDGEMENTS

I spoke to over a hundred people in researching this book. It was a fascinating and invigorating experience.

In particular, the people at Panorama welcomed me, gave this book the research base it needed and made me laugh. Special thanks to Simon Grigg for the introduction and Justin Fleming for his broadminded approach and for open access to the people there.

From that grounding within Tour Operation, moving across and around, the people who have opened up to me have been astounding. Some prefer their words to appear anonymously but, to all, a huge Thank You.

Joanna Grigg
September 2000

CONTENTS

INTRODUCTION

Travel's an exciting business. The product is glamorous and the whole industry is growing and changing so fast even insiders can't keep up. And loads of people want to work in the travel business because ... well, because working in travel takes you nearer to travelling, even if you are deskbound; because working in travel can mean doing a lot of travelling yourself or living abroad. But it's also because there's an atmosphere in the industry quite unlike anywhere else: an enthusiasm (of people working with a product they are passionate about), an of-course-we-can attitude and, above all, a congregation of people who, broadly, like to be with other people.

Because the travel industry is a service industry (it doesn't make things, it rearranges them) and is based around the travelling customers and their needs, you won't succeed in it unless you, too, like to be with people. It's also a young industry – if you're a bit wrinkly you may get funny looks. All this adds up to a unique atmosphere, so it's easy to forget that the travel industry is there to make money. You need to have a commercial head on your shoulders, to want to understand the 'business' of the business and to see how you can put excellent customer service alongside profit-making enterprise. So it's a shame that travel pays so badly: it's recognised as a lousy way to make a fortune, except for the occasional few. But for most people, that's not what it's about.

It's a massive business: people say that one in nine people worldwide work in travel and tourism, including two million of us in the UK. It has such a broad definition that it can include entertainers, sportspeople, beach cafés and many businesses that rely on tourism, so it will never be precisely quantifiable. But what everyone agrees on is that it's huge, and growing. It isn't the most stable of industries: margins are tight and travel fashions change. Businesses constantly evolve to meet customer needs, so you'll have to be adaptable, to watch for change and work towards the next exciting opportunity. But if you want to work in travel, you'll be that sort of person anyway.

So what's it like once you're in this travel business?

Is it
● the most exciting place to be in this new high-leisure, new-technology era?
● the fast-moving and glamorous end of the service industry?
● reaching the far corners of the globe ... and beyond?
● making room for entrepreneurs and high-fliers galore, a way to untold riches?

or is it
● full of insecure, poorly paid, grungy jobs where you never unpack and have no indication of what the future holds?

The answer is both. This book looks at the travel business through the eyes of the people who work in it. It is based on conversations with dozens of people, distilling their comments on what they really think about their work and the future. More than that, it's a summary of who they are, because people in travel are not normal. They range from 'fun' to 'mad'. Even accountants party. 'It's not a job, it's a way of life' is the usual line. Oh yeah? But the more you discover, the more you see that this is true. Talk to some of the people who live for the immediacy, the glamour, the fact that nothing is ever the same for more than three seconds, the extremely hard work which brings great personal rewards and constant contact with people, and if you identify with them, go for it – it's a great place to be.

This book is entitled *How to Make It in the Travel Industry*. What does 'make it' mean? If it's dosh you're after, then become an accountant (in travel, if you like – there are high-earning people in travel). But in researching this book, and trying to understand why everyone has been so friendly, approachable and good to work with, I finally came to understand that for many people in travel, money is not a priority. For many it's a lifestyle thing. The travel business gives them the chance to live their lives as they choose: in the sun, or away from the nine-to-five, or surrounded by great people, or doing something they're really interested in. They won't get rich but, by gum, they'll have a great time. And for them, that's making it.

Most travel business jobs are in here, in broad terms at least (one job can have half a dozen titles and vary from one organisation to the next).

A description of each of these jobs forms the main part of the book. They are listed alphabetically (see Contents). Some jobs only take a couple of pages to describe, others go on much longer. This is because you are probably most interested in the large-intake jobs which you can go into as a new boy or new girl. But there are other less obvious ways in, which are also described, as are jobs to help you think farther ahead, and to sound knowledgeable at interview.

There are plenty of side issues in the travel business, especially at the moment. So there are four extra bits at the end. Appendix 1 looks at the structure and current state of the business and lists addresses and publications you might find useful; appendix 2 looks at careers and getting a job; appendix 3 looks at qualifications you might consider getting at some point and appendix 4 gives a list of website addresses you might want to look at.

And that's it. It's a taster of the business and a starting point for more research. Plenty of the roles described are covered in more depth in specialist books. Go on-line, too, and look at travel websites. Walk into your local travel agency and talk to the people there. Ditto your tourist information office and your local tourist attraction – talk to anyone you know who has contacts with the business. That enthusiasm is what's going to make the difference and will launch your career in the right direction.

ACCOUNTANT

Accountants get everywhere. They are the back-room people of every industry, and as they speak 'financial' they are the links with the money people and the City. In travel, as the industry grows and gets more attention from the world's businesspeople, so the entrepreneurs (the original travellers who created the businesses – see Entrepreneur section) are increasingly being replaced at high levels by accountants.

This ain't such good news for the entrepreneurs, but if you want a solid training and qualification and also work in a whizzy industry, this could be the thing for you.

There are various types of accountants, differing in the training they do and where they do it, and in the roles they perform. In travel, it's mainly management accountants who run the finances of businesses such as airlines, travel agencies and tour operators. These businesses range in size from tiny, requiring only a part-time person to keep the books, to those requiring humongous financial departments with scores of people and a highly structured career ladder. Within these departments are specialist areas where people concentrate on different parts of the accounts processes: invoicing, credit control or whatever.

You can divide the roles into two types: transaction processing and information creation. At certain times of year, and especially at the financial year-end, these departments co-operate more than usual to produce monthly and annual figures. If you want to train in departments like these you'll see the workings of the whole accounts process, and gain good all-round experience. Then, when you're in charge, you'll get involved in functions such as managing the accounts team, writing profit forecasts and helping to set overall company policy.

Simon Grigg is a chartered accountant who trained in a firm of practising accountants doing audit work, and moved across to join his present company, the Panorama Holiday Group, seven years ago. He is now its financial director. When he joined it was a relatively small, privately owned tour operator. It now carries ten times the number of passengers and is part of the Airtours group. He has steered the financial side through these changes. 'It's fun,' he says. 'It's challenging. The travel business is fast-moving, and tour operating is a fun industry. The problems are unpredictable, and there's a lot of making and evolving of policy, more than in other industries. This is because travel is changing all the time; it's a very competitive environment and general economic influences have quite a bearing on travel, such as consumer confidence, the value of sterling, and international situations.'

Within the Airtours group, many of the top players are now accountants: why is this? 'Because the management of a successful tour-operating business is dependent on the analysis of numbers,' says Simon. 'If you want to get to the top in travel, train as an accountant.'

THE WORK

Simon's responsibilities include managing the department: 'I have five people report to me, who direct a total team of thirty, and I'm also responsible for everything financial in the company. For example, the accounting for excursion income in resort; the production of monthly management accounts, which tell us whether our business is running according to plan; the production of information which goes to our parent company; the communication of that information, mainly by e-mail but also by business update presentations.

'Communication with the parent company takes up about a quarter of my time. This comes in many forms, such as formal budget presentations and informal last-minute information requests. And not necessarily just financial things: for instance, I deal with comments on the internal audit of resort health and safety procedures, made by the health and safety director and the customer services department.'

The people Simon reports to are all accountants, and those reporting to him are either qualified, or qualified by experience. He also communicates sideways to non-accountants: 'My role here is forming policy at fortnightly board meetings. I have input into decisions that are not my area, and if it's financial, I decide it. My job is more about converting numbers to words than dealing with numbers.'

Within his department, the transaction processing work is very similar to that of any other business. It includes credit control, payroll, expenses, and so on. The only unusual aspect is that the work is multilingual. 'Languages are a definite advantage,' Simon explains. 'We've just recruited a Greek-speaking accountant for the new Greek side of our operation, Manos Holidays. Though most people in the department don't have another language.'

The information creation part of

the work is management accounting. For this, you have to understand the travel business and find your way around information systems other than accountancy. You have to respond to the information demands of the business, and these frequently change. For instance, recent changes include the increasing number of cheap offers in travel agents' windows. These are funded by the tour operators, and accountants have to find a way of controlling these transactions and generating information about them.

'It's more interesting here than in a standard industry,' says Simon. 'That's why I've stayed.'

SKILLS YOU'LL NEED

'Intellect,' says Simon. 'You need to be very committed and work hard. Be quick-thinking, because things are changing so fast. IT-literate, accurate, numerate, and literate. You need to be able to string words together, put a good argument together and write in a form to suit the recipient. To succeed, you need to be a communicator, have leadership skills, and have a broad view about travel and the industry.'

PRACTICAL INSIDER INFORMATION ON HOW TO GET THE JOB

'Take a year out as a rep to learn the product,' advises Simon. 'Though after A levels you're too young to rep, generally, so I'd recommend going to university first. You can't progress unless you're a graduate. You have to milk the education system as well as you can and exit it as late as possible.

You've got to decide what you want to do. If you want to get on, identify your ability and you can go a long way. If you're a graduate, train with one of the Big Six accountancy firms, qualify and join a travel company. This is because your training, within the audit function, centres on analysis, and will equip the brightest people to think in an analytical way, and translate those thoughts for the non-accountant.'

Travel companies also take trainees into their accounts departments, or into general training schemes where they can choose to spend some time in accounts. 'Some people don't achieve their full potential when they do their A levels. It's much harder for people training here in the department to get to the top, but it's not impossible, and the chances are that people coming to train in my department have chosen not to go down the university/ chartered route. If they are able, and do CIMA [the management accountant qualification], that won't preclude them from getting to the top.'

ADMINISTRATOR

'It's a big, big area,' says a travel insider about the administrative support in holiday resorts. Another place to be a travel 'admin' is within a travel agency, though the administration here is sometimes handled by the sales consultants themselves. If not, there'll be an admin person for every four or five salespeople.

There are admin roles within every large organisation, and if you're the right sort of person with the necessary qualities to do well, and the ambition to move on, you can make this the beginning of a career in travel without too many paper qualifications.

First, though, if you're going to be an admin, why not do it in style, and live in the sun? This is what Tracy Turki does: 'I originally started as a kiddie rep,' she says. 'Then a position came free and I became a rep, then head rep. Then I had my son and became an administrator in the office.' (See Children's representative, Holiday representative sections.)

As a resort manager explains: 'Reps enjoy the contact with the customers but after several years and the continued questions that people ask you, plus the hours that a rep works compared to an admin, you feel you want more of a normal timescale. As a rep the hours are twenty-four hours a day, seven days a week. As an admin it's more structured. You'll go in and have a list of tasks and activities to do and you'll usually do them within certain hours. There's lots of people contact on the phone, not face to face so much.'

Tracy's work involves the day-to-day administration of Panorama's holidays in her resort, Hammamet in Tunisia. 'There are three of us in the office. We look after the reservations through to any changes in the resort, through to organising departures: the list is endless. It takes over your life, because you can't say "That's it, I'm off". If someone's broken their leg and they're in a foreign clinic you've got to reassure them, explain the procedure and organise things.'

The work is very varied: reps are reliant on information from lots of different people and organisations and their main link with the outside world is the admin. You supply the rooming lists, tell reps which guests are coming to their hotels, and generally support them. If a rep has a problem with the **unit** you'll help them switch the guest to alternative accommodation.

'Over the years as a rep you work with some excellent admins,' says the resort manager. 'And some that aren't perhaps as good as you'd like them to be. If an admin makes a mistake with the arrivals, people can get missed: if a rep has a list of twenty people and really there are twenty-two, if those two people are the last to come through then the rep would go without them. The other thing that can happen, if the admins don't check the **manifests** against all the arrivals, is that the reps go to the airport thinking there are only twenty people but twenty-two arrive. It can be very embarrassing. Guests could come out and say "Hello, I'm here" and the rep can't find them on the list. The guests' first reaction is to think that you don't know about the booking, that there's no accommodation, and all the anxieties that come with that. A good admin can stop all that happening. The reliability of the information that the reps work with should always be one hundred per cent accurate. They are a very important part of the link: they can influence that first

impression when the guests arrive. You never get a second chance to make that first impression, and although the reps are there, professional and smart, if they've got duff information then it falls at the first hurdle.'

Other admins work within travel agencies. Travel consultants – the people who meet, greet and sell to customers coming into the shops – might do some or all of their own administration. This can include filling in forms, calling the customer to check details, receiving tickets near the date of travel, dispatching tickets, checking details on invoices, typing letters, sending out **confirmations** and so on. But in some agencies there are also people specifically employed to handle the bulk, or even all, of this. Amanda Whitaker is one of these people. She is assistant sales administration manager at a Holiday Hypermarket. Unusually for an agency, the administration department is completely separate from the sales department, leaving the salespeople to get on with their side of the work without any distractions. Amanda describes how it works: 'Here, the girls sell the holidays and we do everything from checking the tickets and confirmations in from the tour operators through to any amendments to the bookings, which can be to dates, resort, who is travelling, etc. This happens quite a lot: some people book on the spur of the moment and then see another resort they'd rather go to, or for some reason can't travel on those dates.

'If there are any complaints about their holiday, customers come to us first. This can be about anything. For instance, people who aren't used to travelling sometimes think their tickets should get there sooner, and can't always understand that their tickets will arrive two weeks before departure. Or for a late booking, that it might not be possible to get their tickets to them and they will have to pick them up at the airport.'

Amanda and her colleagues also take payments for holidays, and sell ancillaries such as ski passes, car hire, airport car parking, even phonecards. She describes the sales part of her role: 'It's easy to sell a holiday, but customers don't necessarily want to buy airport parking, and they don't want to spend even more money. You have to tell them the pros of it.' Not all admins in agency work have this amount of customer contact, or a sales role, although there will always be some customer contact, in case of queries. Much of this will be by phone.

PEOPLE WHO DO IT

'It's difficult for a travel agency to get admin staff,' explains Amanda. 'Most people with travel agency experience wouldn't want to do an admin role, and if you want to do admin, other industries are better paid. Most people would hope to move over to the sales side, though that move is quite difficult.' Tour operators also find it difficult to get admin staff with travel experience. 'Many resort admins are former reps,' says an insider, 'but it's not always possible to find good ex-reps to do the work, and many tour companies employ people with administrative experience, but no

travel experience, to go out to resort.'

WHAT IT'S LIKE

Amanda describes how she feels about her work: 'I do like it; it's very challenging because it's very busy. There's quite a lot of customer contact. It's nice working with the public; however, working in this department you don't get the opportunity to build such a rapport with customers as you do in sales. And it can be stressful, and the hours aren't great: people work two weekends in three. But there's a good atmosphere and good teamwork. If you don't want that nine-to-five then this is a good option for you.

'Travel's not as glamorous as you'd think: when you're younger you think it's going to be really exciting and that you'll go on lots of trips. But it is interesting in that I've learned a lot and it has encouraged me to travel more.

'As assistant manager I oversee the department and make sure it runs smoothly. I do the rotas and appraisals, look at training needs, do the training where I can, or find training, and encourage staff to meet sales targets.'

Tracy also enjoys her role, partly for the chance to work and live abroad: 'When it's your day off and you're sitting on the beach, it's quite rewarding that you can live this lifestyle. It wouldn't have the same appeal in England: part of the appeal is that it's overseas.' Does she like it? 'The day that I stop liking it will be the day that I close the door and leave.'

SKILLS YOU'LL NEED

As some of the tasks can be

monotonous, you need to be patient and able to keep your mind on a task. You must be extremely organised, and able to use or willing to be trained in using computer systems. You must also be numerate, literate and tidy. There's a lot of responsibility: it takes people who get things right.

Where the role has customer contact, you need to be patient, and have an outgoing personality to cope with people you wouldn't necessarily want to talk to under different circumstances. When you are selling ancillaries, you need to be a good organiser, as you're helping to plan someone's trip: you need to suggest things they will need, and also need to develop sales skills.

The role of admin in resort is changing. A lot of people still start as reps then go into admin, but with advances in technology tour operators need people who have computer and office skills as well as administrative skills. These people also need a language because they're dealing with suppliers and have to be able to converse in the local language.

PRACTICAL INSIDER INFORMATION ON HOW TO GET THE JOB

Contact tour operators and travel agency groups and ask for their recruitment packs. Ask at your local travel agencies and scan the local papers for vacancy details. Remember that there is administrative work within all organisations, and that this can be a good way in before you apply to move sideways into your preferred role.

You need to show that you have the qualities they are looking for. Highlight any admin work you have done at school or college, perhaps for a club, or during Saturday or vacation work.

Remember to ask what training and back-up you'll get: you'll certainly need on-the-job guidance to start with. One resort recruiter says that 'part of their training is a matter of them coming out and seeing things on the front line. They see things such as what could happen with an overbooking, or people arriving they didn't know about, as a result of them not doing something.' Employers will provide full initial and on-going training programmes.

GLOSSARY
● **Confirmations**
Notices sent by the tour operators to their clients via agencies when they have accepted a booking and deposit, but before the tickets are sent out.
● **Unit**
Unit of accommodation, i.e. apartment, hotel room, etc.
● **Manifest**
A list of the people on a flight. Tour operators supply them for their charter flights, and these should tally with the airline's own manifests.

AGENCY SALES (IN TOUR OPERATION)

TRAVEL RATING: 8/10. You sell the benefits of your product (package holidays) to travel agents, so you have to be familiar with your destinations and take clients out there.

MONEY: As it's a sales job, hence target-driven, money can be very good. Probably starting on £15–20,000 plus **commission**.

HOURS: Some nine-to-five, but mostly gallivanting.

HEALTH RISK: 5/10 if you can hold your booze and a conversation at the same time; 10/10 if you then try to drive your company car.

PRESSURE RATING: 7/10. Sales is a pressurised occupation but it's a great product to sell.

GLAMOUR RATING: 8/10. You travel and meet lots of interesting people.

*Tour operators sell mainly through travel agents: these agents need to understand and like a holiday product before they will sell it to their customers. **Account managers** and their staff in the agency sales departments of tour operators promote their brand to travel agents.*

Their key roles are to agree **commission** rates, sign the deals with the **multiples** and **independents** and, once the deals are signed, support these agents' education and development through visits, arranging conferences and **educationals**, and so on. They also liaise should there be any problems: they are the main point of contact between agents and tour operators.

Agency salespeople devise all sorts of methods to draw agents' attention to their holidays. One account manager says: 'We organise a number of conferences each year where essentially we put on a cabaret – we try to show the agents the benefits of our holidays.' They follow this type of activity with calls, visits and mailshots, as well as offers of educational trips. These may be given to the sales consultants within the agencies who sell the greatest number of holidays to a given destination, say. This has a dual purpose: it acts as an incentive for travel agents to sell as many of these holidays as possible. It also increases agents' knowledge of the holidays: a travel agent who has been to a particular destination and a certain hotel, and enjoyed it, will talk more convincingly about it to the customer afterwards.

SKILLS YOU'LL NEED

'They are salespeople through and through,' says a recruiter. 'They come into it because they are salespeople, but instead of selling cars they take their agents overseas.' There is also an element of PR in the role, so any experience you can get there is a bonus. See more specialist information on sales careers for a breakdown of the skills and experience you need. In a nutshell, though, travel salespeople are extremely determined and competitive, outgoing, have all-round communication skills (selling is as much about listening as it is about talking), are gregarious, and love standing up in front of people and performing. They are target-driven, enjoy travelling and living out of hotel rooms, and get on with anybody.

PRACTICAL INSIDER INFORMATION ON HOW TO GET THE JOB

Agency salespeople are in great demand at the moment. As one tour operator puts it: 'The two areas that have gone through a complete metamorphosis in this industry in the last few years have been product purchasing (contracting), and **distribution**. The travel agencies' merging has been critical, and salaries in field sales, out on the road, are very high.' It's not an area you can go straight into, though. You will need to have a 'proven track record' in travel sales (that's industry-speak for having been a good salesperson over a period of time). This could be in a travel agency or with a tour operator, perhaps starting as a rep or in the call centre and proving your sales ability then working your way up.

GLOSSARY

● **Account managers**

Senior salespeople who are responsible for one or a number of clients or 'accounts'. This has nothing to do with accountancy work, where senior people are called accounts managers (note the extra 's').

● **Commission**

Each holiday sold by a travel agent earns the agent money in commission. A typical industry rate is 10 per cent of the cost of the holiday. There is no further cost to the traveller. This is how agents make their money.

● **Distribution**

Another word for sales. It means distributing the product to the marketplace.

● **Educationals**

Educational trips organised by tour operators and given or sold at low cost to travel agents. This first-hand experience of destinations encourages agents to sell holidays there. Tour operators' own staff also go on educationals to give them first-hand experience of the product. Educationals used to be given in rotation to staff but increasingly they are given as incentives.

● **Independents**

Travel agents that have held out and refused to be bought up by the multiples. Some may have a number of agencies in different towns but none are anywhere near as large as the multiples.

● **Multiples**

Chains of travel agents usually owned by the large holiday groups. Although none is supposed to sell holidays from their owner organisation in preference to those of their competitors, this is a fine line to police. The public usually don't understand that the large travel agencies are owned by organisations that also run tour operators.

AIRLINE CABIN CREW

Cabin crew (formerly air hostesses, trolley dollies, air stewards and stewardesses, known in the trade as main crew) look after passengers on a flight. They do everything from adhering to safety regulations and dealing with rude and even violent passengers to serving food and drinks, selling goods and clearing puke.

More unusual flights might mean looking after an unaccompanied minor, talking aircraft noises through with someone who is terrified of flying, arranging a comfortable flight for somebody with special needs, handcuffing a violent passenger or administering CPR (electric shock treatment) to someone who has suffered a heart attack. Oh yes, and two babies were born on BA flights last year, and guess who delivered them ...?

The everyday reality, though, is that this is a customer service job: passengers arrive on your aircraft expecting a safe and comfortable flight, and it's your task to provide it. Whatever those airline disaster movies in the seventies taught us, most flights don't crash or erupt into **air rage**: most include a good cross-section of friendly, interesting people going away for various reasons. Some (such as the night flight to Ibiza) might have a special type of clientele where you have to look out for particular problems. **Charter** airlines are more likely to carry noisy, excited and even obnoxious people than the standard set of businesspeople and independent travellers usually found on **scheduled** flights.

Talking to people who fly, what comes through time and time again is that it isn't a job, it's a lifestyle. The money's not bad but you won't get rich. The job varies according to the airline and the type of customers you look after, and isn't in itself exciting most of the time. It is very busy, so there's no time to get bored. But most people do it primarily for the perks: the travel and the whole atmosphere of working with like-minded people.

THE JOB

Tonny Madsen works for BA on its **short-haul** scheduled flights out of Heathrow. He says: 'I love my job; it's what I always wanted to do.' On a typical day he arrives at the airport in uniform and reports to the centre for flight deck and cabin crew. He checks the safety notices and updates himself on safety equipment procedures, then chats with crew he's flown with before. 'Then the flight crew introduce themselves,' he says, 'and we answer safety and first aid questions. They tell you about the day's flight, who's on board and the **service**, and ask who wants to work where on the aircraft. After briefing you go for your transport, which is the bus that takes you out to the aircraft. We go through security at the briefing room, so we don't need to be checked again.'

Once on the aeroplane he checks the safety equipment and searches for any items that shouldn't be there. 'Sometimes they put on packages for us to find,' he explains, 'just to make sure we're doing our job properly.' Then he starts preparing the galleys,

checks how many meals there are on board, and how many special meals. This all takes ten or fifteen minutes.

Then passengers start boarding. 'We give out newspapers,' explains Tonny, 'and spread out through the cabin. It takes about twenty minutes to get people seated. Then it's time for **pushback**. We've already started our safety demonstrations by then. We check all the passengers are strapped in, seats are back, bags stowed away properly and so on, and sit down for take-off.'

In the air, it's time for the trollies: there's a set procedure for cabin service on each flight, and Tonny and the crew serve drinks, meals, sky-high shopping and anything else that's needed. 'We deal with any emergencies aboard the aircraft,' he says. 'You get people with asthmatic attacks, diabetes, heart attacks. Travel is quite stressful on the body and people react in different ways. Occasionally, a child is born on board the aircraft too: I wouldn't like to deliver a baby, but I could. We ask on the PA if there's a doctor or medical people on board.'

SCHEDULED VS CHARTER

There is a difference between working scheduled flights, as Tonny does, and charter flights. Barry, a 'Number 1' or supervisor for a major charter airline, describes how his work differs from Tonny's: 'Our passengers are different: they're at the lower end of the market. We carry holiday passengers, who are normally families. But some of our passengers don't seem to think you're human.' He describes what can happen: 'A passenger might scream at you for things in a way that they wouldn't in a restaurant. If there's a beef meal, for instance, they might say: "I don't eat beef," then go completely berserk for half an hour because that's all there is.' So are the image and the reality different? 'Airline work is perceived to be all glamour and glitz,' says Barry. 'There are glamorous parts, such as a week in Jamaica all expenses paid. The job itself is not. There's not a lot of brainwork involved, and every flight is virtually the same. Even though every day you have different passengers, you're doing the same job.'

When small problems arise on Barry's charter flights, such as the **IFE** not working, there's less scope to sort it out because the flight is likely to be full, with no spare seats to move passengers to. Barry feels that things are changing for the worse: 'Passengers know more, and want more for nothing. For instance, we give out newspapers on the way home, then people ask for different newspapers then tut or shake their heads when we haven't got them. People see the image and the uniform, but that's all people see. We're groomed to look smart all the time but the reality is crawling around on the floor with sick bags and nappies. We're like swans, elegant on the outside but underneath paddling like mad to keep up.'

Flying's a good industry to be in, but it's a very specific lifestyle that people either love or hate. 'You'll put up with the crap for the perks,' is how Barry puts it. 'I wouldn't change what

I do because of the hours I work and the pay, and I like to travel. I get four or five holidays a year. You are just a glorified waiter if you don't want to travel.'

But cabin crew on both sides of the industry have something in common: 'I could never imagine doing anything else,' says Tonny. 'It's a fantastic job – I love it. You might have a problem for an hour or two hours, and work hard, then your problem is gone. In an office it can go on for weeks.' Barry agrees: 'The parties and lifestyle lead to burn-out though the work itself isn't too pressured. Young people who fly tend to party hard. It's a great lifestyle but people move to scheduled for a more normal life.'

SAFETY

The safety element of the work is extremely important and quite different to most other customer service work. Much of the initial training course concentrates on standard safety procedures and what to do in emergencies. All crew are required to take annual safety and first aid exams to ensure that their knowledge is up to date. These are multiple-choice exams taken on the computer, so you don't need academic ability to pass them.

UNIFORM AND GROOMING

Image is all-important in this job. You'll be given several sets of uniform and need to arrive for work looking pristine. This means different things with different employers but always includes for women at least a minimum of make-up, hair well cut, naturally coloured and above shoulder length, or tied back, nails polished or buffed, and for everyone being generally well groomed.

CAREER PROGRESSION

On a **long-haul** flight there may be up to fourteen cabin crew members. Barry is a **Number 1**: 'I am a cabin supervisor or Number 1, which is the equivalent to a **Cabin Services Director (CSD)** in scheduled. You're there to organise events such as the safety briefing before you go on board. You set the service for the day and make sure it runs smoothly. You're in charge of on-board communications between ground staff and captain and aircrew.' It normally takes a minimum of five years before you'll be promoted to this level. 'We're all trained exactly the same in terms of safety,' says Barry. 'The more senior members of the team will be called on to sort out any problems that the main crew can't.'

Some flights will have a **purser** as well as a CSD: the purser is in charge of the economy cabin, and is called a **Number 2** in charter. There might be up to four pursers on a long-haul scheduled aircraft, one for each cabin: first class, upper-deck club, lower-deck club and economy. With most airlines you can apply to be a purser after two years.

From there, some people choose to stop flying and work in an office. If you do, and you work for a large airline, you may not have to leave because they are vast organisations: there's a role for you somewhere in marketing, recruitment, and so on.

Tonny did a stint in cabin crew recruitment: 'It's nice to get out there once in a while; you realise how lucky you are to be flying. I did recruitment for three months last year. The people were lovely but I couldn't cope with the nine-to-five. Our working hours are just so flexible. People don't tend to leave flying, or only because they are moving away. A lot of people start by saying "I'm only here for six months" and twenty years later they're still flying. I've heard of people who've taken retirement and found it really, really hard. Once it's in your blood you can't get out of it.'

BEFORE YOU APPLY

Some charter airlines find it difficult to get enough good staff, especially in the South, where there is more competition from other airlines. The more prestigious scheduled airlines tend to have waiting lists, and may even go through the recruitment procedure and then put people on hold before they have the vacancies to allow them to start work. As in the rest of the travel business, airlines are affected by economic and other trends: the Gulf War was disastrous for all aspects of the industry, but the newly buoyant economy in the Far East is a good sign.

Although recruitment trends vary, airlines cannot afford to take people unless they are completely up to the job. Hopeful cabin crew are often initially told: 'We like you, but you need more customer service experience. Try again in a couple of years.' Some people become holiday representatives to gain that experience, as the job is similar in many ways. Others start as ground staff. Tonny advises: 'Get inside the airline, get the customer service experience. It's quite similar work except for the emergency side.' He also advises you to start with a charter airline: 'It's good experience. You'll think it's a doddle to work for BA after charter.' Barry agrees: 'If you go into it as a career you're better going into charter: there are younger people and it's more fun. Scheduled people are more graveyard; charter crew are probably aged twenty to thirty-five, but in scheduled more like twenty-five to fifty-five.'

TRAINING

Cabin crew is a demanding role where you need to be committed and prepared to continue learning throughout your career. The initial training will last probably five or six weeks and will entail everything from customer service skills and cultural awareness issues to safety and emergency procedures. You need to do well in your training to go on with the work; some people leave at this stage. With BA you train for five and a half weeks. 'A lot of it is about safety on board the aircraft,' says Tonny, 'what to do if there's a fire, how to get passengers out of the aircraft on the slides, and so on. Another thing is first aid, how to help people who are ill. It's a very hard, non-residential course. You have to give up your life for five and a half weeks, forget about parties. A few people fail the training course and that's because they're not giving it one hundred per cent.'

THE PERKS

People fly for the perks: you get great concessions on flights when you're on leave, as does your partner. But these are on stand-by, so if the plane's full you have to wait for the next one, and the next one, and the next one. It can take a week to get home from some long-haul destinations; short haul is usually easier as there are so many flights going each day. Once on, you may well be upgraded to better seats and service, into the club-class cabin, say.

Some airlines also have married rosters where they will put staff with their partners if both work for the airline. If you get a week waiting around in Jamaica with your partner, life can't be all that bad.

There is also free car parking at airports, subsidised food, discount car hire and a range of other discounts.

SKILLS YOU'LL NEED

● You need to get on with anyone and to work as part of a team, to be level-headed, thick-skinned, warm, able to hold a conversation naturally, able to work with others.
● You need common sense, an open-minded, flexible approach, a 'can do' attitude, the ability to keep smiling.
● Punctuality is extremely important: if you're even one minute late you can't check in.
● Usually a minimum of twelve months' customer service experience. This can be anything from bar work to police work.
● Flexibility: you need to be happy to work anywhere, any time. You need to be prepared to be away for

Christmas and bank-holidays, and whatever your religion you need to work with, and serve, alcohol.

● Minimum age 19 or 20. Some airlines like younger people; others don't have upper age limits though retire you early.

● You need to be within a broad ratio of weight to height, though BA 'don't just take skinny people – we take all sorts if they're good'. Some airlines may judge you more on your looks. Minimum five foot two, maximum six foot two is usual.

● You need to be able to relate to people from all ethnic and cultural backgrounds, both as colleagues and passengers.

● A language, necessary with some airlines but not with others.

● You have to live near the airport (BA stipulates a maximum hour and a half land travelling time from the airport).

PRACTICAL INSIDER INFORMATION ON HOW TO GET THE JOB

● Write to all relevant airlines and read their recruitment packs carefully. You'll get a feel for the type of personality as well as the skills they are looking for. Most people start in charter, often with smaller airlines. You'll stand a better chance of getting the job if you assess your skills and experience and apply to the right organisations.

● Airlines vary in their recruitment procedures. Some judge applicants solely on total scores after answering standard questions. This eliminates interviewer bias. As one recruiter says: 'We're all different; just because you don't like someone doesn't mean they can't do the job.' Others look more closely at personality and how it fits the airline's image.

● All will preselect on the basis of the application form. Study the literature and forms carefully and ensure that you write what they want to hear: become their ideal cabin crew member and tell them about yourself.

● If you're successful with the application form you'll attend a day's interview session, with a group interview. This will include exercises such as having to advertise and sell one interviewee's home town as a tourist attraction. You need to show you can work as part of a team. Other exercises will test your customer service skills and other aptitudes.

● Selection will also include a two-to-one interview where you can ask and answer questions about the work and yourself. You'll be interviewed by someone from the recruitment department as well as a current cabin crew member.

● There will be sight and medical tests, and if you are applying with a language there will be a language test. If it's not clear, phone to find out when these tests will take place.

● If you don't get the job first time around it may be because you don't yet have enough experience. If it's not already been explained to you, phone and ask what the recruiter suggests you do before you reapply.

GLOSSARY

● **Air rage**
Tabloid-coined term for some passengers' angry behaviour on flights.

● **Cabin Services Director (CSD)
(or Number 1 on charter)**
Cabin crew member in charge of the
team.

● **Charter**
Airlines and flights that carry
passengers on package tours. There
are more passengers on a charter
than on a scheduled aircraft: 757s
carry a maximum of 180 passengers
in full economy scheduled, while the
same craft on charter could carry 233
people.

● **IFE**
In-flight entertainment.

● **Long-haul**
Flights lasting more than
approximately five hours.

● **Purser (or Number 2)**
Second in charge after the CSD.

● **Pushback**
When the aircraft is pushed back
ready for taxiing to the runway and
take-off.

● **Scheduled**
Airlines and aircraft carrying
independent travellers, often
businesspeople, people who have
organised their own holidays or are
going to visit relatives, etc. Some
package tour passengers fly scheduled.
Passengers expect better service on
these flights; there are more crew per
passenger, and there's more legroom.

● **Service**
The order in which the meal, drinks
and shopping are presented to the
passenger, and the process of doing
this.

● **Short-haul**
Flights lasting less than around five
hours.

AIRLINE GROUND STAFF

TRAVEL RATING: 0–6/10. There's a whole range of possibilities depending on your job and employer.

MONEY: Again, varies enormously – handling agents are known for their bad pay, airlines for their better pay and conditions.

HOURS: Mostly shift work – some long shifts but often the chance to move these to create blocks of travel time.

HEALTH RISK: 4/10. Long hours in air-conditioned, sunlight-free areas. Occasional abusive customers.

PRESSURE RATING: 5/10. It gets easier once you've learned to deal with long queues of stressed travellers.

GLAMOUR RATING: 5/10. Smart uniform, an occasional chance to meet famous people; otherwise, not really.

*Working for an airline or **handling agent**, ground staff do the airport-based work needed to get people on board their flights and the flights off to their destinations.*

Airports process millions of people each year, and huge numbers of support staff work within the airport to help them get on to the right flight at the right time. These ground staff are employed either by the airport itself or by airlines or agents. There are hundreds of different jobs, and job titles vary in the different organisations. This section looks at a few of the more visible ones: ticket sales, **check-in** and flight connections.

THE WORK

Annette Matthews is an experienced member of British Airways' ground staff. She worked at other airports, for both an airline and a handling agent, before starting her current job. She works in a number of functions, including at the flight connections desk, where, she says: 'You're there to help people who are connecting onwards if they haven't been able to check through to their connecting flight.' Annette explains that passengers don't have to go **landside** if they're travelling from one international to another, or if they're transferring from a domestic to an international flight. They can remain **airside**. This job is based airside and entails checking people in if they're transferring. When flights come in late, however, and people miss their connections, she's there to rebook, reroute or provide hotel accommodation. This is known as customer service recovery for people whose journey has developed a glitch. 'It's a huge thing when flights come in late, with three hundred people on board,' says Annette, 'and perhaps half have missed their connections. Aircraft can't normally wait for passengers delayed by their incoming flights. Airlines are very much into punctuality, and getting planes off on time, especially nowadays.'

There are also flight connection hosts, who will meet people with tight connections off flights and escort them to the next flight, as well as a specialist team of tactical managers. These managers use the computer to monitor all flights in and out of the airport. This tells them how many people will miss their flights. By the time passengers reach Annette, they've already been rebooked. It's then up to her to sort out the tickets and explain the situation.

'That's the worst place I work because passengers are already tired,' says Annette. 'You get a lot of hassle down there. I'm either doing nothing or when it's busy it's awful because half an aircraft has missed their connections. I arrange cars or buses to Heathrow and, if they are rebooked on to a different carrier, arrange tickets. This is all under time pressure.'

The other part of the airport where Annette works is landside at the ticket desk: 'Its main function is for people coming to pick up tickets. It's also used as a problem-solving desk for people who are changing flights, have lost their tickets, forgotten their passports, or have no visas. We can tell them where to go to get a new passport or visa, and rearrange their flights. On a lot of tickets there's a charge for changing them, so I take money too.'

Annette already had a ticketing qualification but underwent an intensive seven-week training course when she joined the airline, covering aspects of ticketing, cultural relations, customer service and more. This training, and experience, enables her to deal with all sorts of passengers:

'People are often panicked: they've missed their flights or got some sort of problem. The ticket desk, customer services and check-in get the worst of the difficult and angry customers. At least once a day you'll have someone who's rude. I'm quite laid back about them, you've got to be, and you've got to like people. If somebody's shouting I ask them to go away and have a cup of tea, calm down and then come back. Some of those who are horrible will apologise afterwards. It can get you down but the people you work with are good, and you're never on your own on a desk. Of course, you also get people who bring you a box of chocolates because you've helped them out.

'It's very interesting meeting so many people going off to so many different places. Solving their problems is interesting, and then sometimes you chat. You meet all cultures, all walks of life. You're learning all the time about different nationalities. I enjoy my work.'

Working in these roles within an airport is like working on board an aircraft as cabin crew or in many other travel roles: if you don't like people, don't even think about it. Most of the people you meet are lovely, and grateful for your help, but as Annette says, you're the passenger's first point of contact in a situation that can be very stressed: people who are late for their flights, or drunk, or obnoxious for no obvious reason. You may be the person they take it out on, and even if they later apologise you've got to be thick-skinned and realise that it's the uniform they're shouting at, not you.

'You're either a customer services person or you're not,' says Annette. 'It's not something you can learn, I believe.'

It's also a team role, and there is always back-up. Training and management support are also very good. Once you are working for and experienced with a good employer you can move around and progress to different jobs: for example, to aircrew or to working abroad, or come off shift work and do a job without customer contact.

Ground staff work is always shift-based, but this is not as frustrating as it sounds: if you are into travel and find an employer with flexible shifts, you can arrange blocks of time off to make the most of the concessionary flights. As Annette says: 'If you like travel and people, then you're sorted, really.'

SKILLS YOU'LL NEED

● You must be level-headed.
● You have to like people and working with people.
● You have to be flexible and able to work shifts, though there are jobs behind the scenes where you can work nine-to-five.
● Look smart. Women don't have to wear lots of make-up but employers are usually strict on hair, which has to be worn up. Earrings must be plain, etc. – each airline has its own policies on this.
● You must be able to cope with pressure.
● Employers like it if you have another language; though they may take you without, it's becoming more and more a bonus to have one.
● You'll need some customer service

experience, but it doesn't matter what this is.
● You don't need specific qualifications but you must be able to operate a computer and have a reasonable head for figures.

PRACTICAL INSIDER INFORMATION ON HOW TO GET THE JOB

The major airlines are often looking for trainee staff, though less commonly for more experienced people, as they like to recruit from within. Write to the airlines based in your area and ask for their vacancy information and recruitment packs. You may see vacancies advertised, or recruitment fairs for a particular airport. These are good places at which to make the right initial impression.

When you are called for interview you may find it's in a group setting as well as one-to-one or two-to-one. You need to show them that you are unflappable, courteous and in control in all situations: not loud and bossy or a wallflower. You need to be confident about why your experience qualifies you for this work: what has it given you that makes you so invaluable? They may give you some examples of difficult situations, so think of some beforehand and talk them over with a friend, working out the best way to deal with them.

Assure them that you are prepared to start at the bottom, work hard at anything and will love the work. And, of course, make sure you look smart.

GLOSSARY

● **Airside**

The other side of security clearance.

● **Check-in**

The desk where passengers present
their tickets and passports to register
for the flight they are booked on to.
The member of staff checks all the
details with computer records, makes
safety checks, may allocate seats, and
accepts luggage for the hold. This is
done before security clearance.

● **Handling agents**

These provide ground staff for airlines
that do not have their own in any
particular airport. Airlines use
handling agents at destination
airports and usually have their own
ground staff at their home airports.
Handling agents are notorious in the
industry for their low pay. The work
is the same as for airline ground staff,
but there are no travel concessions.

● **Landside**

Any airport areas accessible before
security clearance.

AIRPORTS

There are scores of airports in the UK, from tiny to gigantic. They need staffing and managing to deliver an excellent service to their customers, to comply with safety regulations and to make money.

There are jobs of almost every description within a large airport. You can work as an electrician, a shopkeeper, a cleaner, a chef, a baggage handler, an air traffic controller, a car park attendant, an operational manager, an accountant ... the list is endless. And many of these jobs need skills that you can switch between sectors. For instance, if you work in retail in the high street, you could make the move across to retail within an airport, just as you could to retailing railway tickets or other travel jobs. So although an airport is a very different work environment, in a lot of roles the work you'll do there isn't so different.

AIRPORT MANAGEMENT

If you want to work in airport management you will be employed by a company such as the British Airports Authority (BAA), which runs a number of airports, including Heathrow, or a smaller company such as Luton Airport. There are also many management roles within the other organisations that operate from airports, as mentioned above, such as retailers, **handling agents** and airlines.

Management for an airport company may be divided into three main areas: the commercial side, finance, and operations. Commercial includes developing new as well as existing business by going out and meeting clients and potential clients (these might be retailers who want to use the airport, or airlines, or other organisations). It also includes property services work, as the airport company is landlord of an enormous site and must manage this. Marketing comes under this role, as do other commercial aspects. It could include some planning and development, though this is usually within the control of financial managers within the company, who also look at the future expansion of the airport, a responsibility including planning permission and environmental issues. Information technology is also a huge area.

The most visible part of airport management is operations. This covers areas such as air traffic control (see below), airfield safety, security, facilities (which means porters, cleaners, etc.), car parks, fire services, marshalling, maintenance, buses, electricity, the medical centre, and many others. Operational duty managers are responsible for all this around the clock. Some airports have separate duty managers for the terminals and for the airfield, say, depending on size and structure.

'My role is a combination of customer service and operational management,' says Bronwen Rihan. She joined Luton Airport as one of a team of five duty managers when the post was created two years ago. She is a graduate with experience of operational management in the textile industry. 'It's a question of keeping things running smoothly,' she says. 'You always have to keep looking ahead. Things can go wrong. For instance, there may be a breakdown in a baggage handling system. I would have to put things into place so that this was still functioning. You need an ability to see through the mess and think laterally, asking: how can I solve this problem?'

EMERGENCY!

One of Bronwen's key functions is to be on hand in case of an aircraft emergency. Then she has to make the decision as to whether to activate incident emergency procedures. 'You're not there to put a fire out yourself,' she explains, 'but to restore the airport to its commercial operation. If a runway is blocked, the airport will get fuller and fuller as more passengers arrive for their flights. You'd liaise with the handling agents, hotels, even the chaplaincy to get people down to walk around and chat to passengers.' Thankfully, in the time Bronwen has been doing the job, she has never had such an emergency.

As well as fielding problems, Bronwen's day-to-day activities include liaising with other departments. 'You need to be knowledgeable, and have an interest in absolutely everything,' she says. 'One minute you could be with an electrician and the next with a passenger who's feeling ill.' She can never turn her back on something that's not 100 per cent. For instance, when she's walking around she might spot a blocked fire exit and need to free it up. 'There's plenty of health and safety work because the public are here,' she explains. 'There might be trip hazards, for instance. You need to be lateral thinking, and you need eyes in the back of your head. If you're handing out vouchers to passengers you need to think: does the café know;

have they made extra food? You need a lot of awareness.'

All sorts of problems can arise, but some shifts are relatively quiet. 'Duty managers don't have anything specific to do unless something special happens. In the meantime I'll be reading, doing project work, in meetings, and so on.'

LIAISON

You don't need to know everything, but you do need to know who can help in a particular situation. 'You need to understand problems,' Bronwen explains, 'and also technical things: when you are talking with technical people, they are the experts, but you need to know what they mean.'

It's very much a liaising, co-ordinating role, which includes gathering information and passing this on to higher management. 'As duty manager, you've not got the responsibility or the budget to make changes, so it can be slightly frustrating sometimes. You need to bridge and liaise, and sometimes you need to be able to bounce back.' Liaison with business partners is also vitally important: these are the other organisations based at the airport. 'If your company needs to do something,' says Bronwen, 'this can have a knock-on to other companies, and you have to negotiate with them. It's so diverse: there's so much to think about; there are so many companies working within one site.'

DECISION-MAKING

Duty managers are in the thick of it. They always need to be helpful, in control and thinking ahead. 'There's a lot of decision-making,' explains Bronwen. 'You also need to be a good negotiator: when you need to shut down a system for maintenance, for instance, you'll need to talk with the electricians and strike a deal with them about covering that situation.' You need to be able to talk to people at all levels, to know when to speak and when to be discreet. You also need high energy levels. For instance, if there's fog or snow or an air traffic controllers' strike, you have an airport full of people and you have to deal with them. Then the loos will flood, perhaps: you have to be able to cope with a lot of diverse situations.

Duty managers also need to be aware of the airport's emergency orders, and how to deal with an emergency situation as laid down by airport control documents. 'You must also be aware of changes to the structure of the airport,' explains Bronwen. 'If you need to get from A to B quickly, you don't want to find somebody's built a wall in the way. I use my quiet periods to go and visit people so I know the layout of the airport.'

There's also a fair amount of responsibility, such as key-holding, or when television crews come to the airport and the duty manager may need to speak to camera.

BEING A MANAGER

Bronwen explains some of the less obvious aspects of her role: 'People see you as "management": sometimes you want to join in with their activities but you must stand on your own. You're straddled between the management and the workforce.

'Shift work isn't easy: you need to be able to cope with this and plan your life around it. Some people love it and never want to go back to normal hours, but it's not for everybody. You don't work any more hours, you just work them differently.

'It can be quite humbling work sometimes, when you have to take the flak and you know the problem is someone else's fault. Sometimes people are so unreasonable. But you can't blame other people: you are the face of the airport.'

TEAMWORK

At Luton Airport there is a team of five duty managers, but only one of these managers is on shift at any one time. So although they rarely work together, they do need to liaise closely. 'With a nine-to-five job you do it, and go home,' explains Bronwen. 'Duty manager is a twenty-four-hour job. I can't go home at two p.m. and say I'll do it tomorrow. I must hand over the relevant information to the next duty manager. The job is rolling twenty-four hours – you cannot make it yours. You need to share information and hold it in your mind, along with its importance, and determine whether it has an impact on the team.' The duty managers write a log, recording everything that has happened on each shift.

'It's a good job to help you learn how to be a team member,' says Bronwen. 'You can benefit and develop yourself from being in a team. In that respect it is really a good job.'

SKILLS YOU NEED AS AN OPERATIONAL DUTY MANAGER

'Getting on with people is very important,' says Bronwen, 'because when things go wrong you all have to work together to ensure that you can recover the situation.' It's not a job for somebody straight from university because you wouldn't have the man-management skills. 'You have to see a bit of the world first,' advises Bronwen, 'understand customer service, and ensure that to people's faces you are always extremely polite and helpful. You bring skills from your first positions into this role.'

It's a fairly isolated role, and therefore not for everybody. You need the confidence to be able to muck in, but also to be able to distance yourself. 'It's a fine line. You need to duck and dive between different roles to achieve an end. I had to send someone home recently because I smelled alcohol on his breath. This person didn't work for my company but his manager didn't want to do it. Sometimes you feel horrible but you know in your heart that it has to be done. You're not always their favourite person, but you know you're respected.'

SKILLS NEEDED FOR AIRPORT MANAGEMENT ROLES GENERALLY

'You need some kind of degree and the ability to translate that energy and knowledge into practice,' says Bina Briggs, human resources officer at Luton Airport. 'The type of degree doesn't matter, though if it's relevant that helps, but we have different graduates doing all sorts of things. There are also certain specific rules within the company. For instance, if it's a marketing vacancy we'd much rather have somebody with something related to marketing.

'Operations people come from all sorts of places,' says Bina. 'A lot of duty managers have good honours degrees and then experience with people within large organisations, and experience of working under some sort of pressure. It's better if it's a related degree. A lot of managers do air transport first degrees.'

A maintenance manager would look after utilities, including the electricity supply for the airport. 'Imagine how much electricity we must use,' comments Bina, 'apart from the obvious lighting on the runways and so on. For instance, the terminal building is full of mechanical systems, conveyor belts, air-conditioning, and so on. In that instance a manager would need a relevant degree. In the medical centre, staff need the relevant qualifications in nursing, occupational health, etc.'

In the main, management roles are advertised outside the airport as well as internally.

AIR TRAFFIC CONTROL

Although the image most of us have of air traffic control is of hazardous runway conditions and tense emergency landings, most air traffic control officers (or ATCOs) in fact work away from airports. There are two main centres in the UK (with a new one being built) where ATCOs known as area controllers stay in constant radio contact with pilots.

Approach controllers take over this contact as the aircraft approach airports. Then contact is passed to aerodrome controllers.

Controlling our airspace is a complex business and is run by NATS (National Air Traffic Services). Their website gives more details about the work, how to train as an ATCO and how to apply. See below for address.

SKILLS YOU'LL NEED TO WORK ANYWHERE IN AN AIRPORT

You have to be over eighteen to work at an airport. This is because most jobs are shift-based and you can't work between the hours of 2200 and 0600 if you are under eighteen.

There's also a medical which everyone working in the airport has to undergo: this is because of Civil Aviation Authority (CAA) regulations. The medical levels are set for each job. For instance, if you're colour-blind you cannot work airside, as everyone airside must be able to help anywhere in an emergency, and many of the emergency procedures rely on being able to identify coloured signals.

'You need to be very flexible and people-orientated,' says Bina Briggs. 'You don't have to like people all the time but you must be able to deal with their needs. It's like a small village, but it's also a business, and we want our customers to come back. If you have a uniform and an ID then your behaviour counts – if you get it wrong, the customer won't fly from that airport again. And, as in any other organisation, you need the marketable skills for that organisation.'

PRACTICAL INSIDER INFORMATION ON HOW TO GET THE JOB

At age sixteen

'It's getting easier for young people,' says Bina. 'If you're coming through a modern apprenticeships scheme or national traineeship, the training organisations are geared up to promoting NVQs [National Vocational Qualifications] relating to the aviation sector. This is a route in. We have a programme here, and get young people after GCSEs in many roles.' These include someone in marketing who finished a national traineeship and stayed on as a marketing assistant, someone training in the car parks, someone in terminal management, a retail trainee who is now a manager, and plenty more. The best way to find out about these schemes is to talk to people at the careers service. 'If all works out, then they are taken on permanently,' says Bina, 'but in the meantime they will gain NVQs in their particular area. They start with the basics of health and safety, using a fax machine, how to answer the phone, and so on, all in a general NVQ for the first six months. Then they go on to NVQs that are relevant to the jobs they are doing. A lot are targeted to the aviation industry.' See Appendix 3.

A level entry

'An airport is a very different environment to an office or the high street,' comments Bina. 'It's a very live environment and it might not suit everybody. "Five minutes" is too late: it's now, now, now all the time.' She recommends that school leavers decide what they want to do and apply for a variety of roles relating to it. 'Try a few things,' she says, 'and see what you think is good.'

Because many British people take a holiday in the sun each summer, most British airports have a summer season. Airports have core staff of permanent people, but to respond to the demands of increased business they take on seasonal staff in all areas. For instance, most handling agents' check-in staff are on temporary contracts to begin with. 'There's quite an opportunity there,' says Bina. 'Also in baggage handling, portering, and so on. Then it becomes like a village with a grapevine: you make contacts and job opportunities come up.'

HOW TO GET WORK

You'll find that there are many different employers within an airport. Some airport companies are huge employers while others **outsource** most activities to other organisations, so you have to apply direct to those. Also, remember that there are other means of travel, each with their own terminals: think about equivalent work with railway companies and in ports.

Research which companies are based at the airport by ringing the information desk, contacting your local JobCentre or visiting the JobCentre on the airport site if there is one. Look in the papers, visit your local library, and find out what the companies do. 'We get hundreds of calls each week,' says Bina, 'asking: "Have you got a job?" I say to them:

"What do you want to do?" They just say: "I want a job." That's not good enough. Call in once you have some sort of idea of what you want to do, and what the company does.'

INSIDER TIPS

Bina gives some advice from her years of experience recruiting at Luton Airport: 'What we need is somebody who can show a little bit of "oomph" and common sense, who can translate their qualification into practice. I've seen thousands of people come through the door, some people with degrees coming out of their ears who can't string two sentences together. They can't sell themselves. If I put them in front of passengers who haven't got what they want they're going to eat them alive. But then sometimes there are people without degrees but with "street cred" who can talk. You need to first research your subject, and then deliver it.

'Personal presentation is very important. Even our cleaners have to be smart. This is a public domain, a stage. What do you do when you're waiting for your plane? You watch. It's a pressurised environment because all the passengers want is to get on that plane. The time between arriving at the airport and getting on that plane is time wasted, and for a lot of people that's anxiety. Intelligent people leave their brains behind on the outskirts of the airport because they're under pressure. They grab the nearest person in uniform. I need somebody who is able to say: "Yes, sir, what would you like?" You must have the gumption to say that, and look smart enough.'

GLOSSARY

● **Handling agent**
A company based at an airport doing things like checking passengers in, dispatching aircraft, etc.

● **Outsource**
To hand over the running of something to another person or organisation.

USEFUL ADDRESSES

For air traffic control information:
● Recruitment Services, National Air Traffic Services Ltd, Room T1213, CAA House, 45–59 Kingsway, London WC2B 6TE. Tel: +44 (0)120 7832 5555. www.nats.co.uk/recruitment
For a good range of aviation links (including UK colleges) try starting at:
● www.midwestav8.com/weblink1.htm

AVIATION PLANNER

The aviation department within a tour company is responsible for buying and controlling the aeroplane seats needed for the holidays. Aviation planners have a similar role to bed contractors (the people who negotiate the accommodation – see Contractor section) in that they need to buy the right amount of the best product at the right price. The rest of the department helps with planning and controlling the whole process of seat buying and putting seats into the system so that they can be sold.

The department starts by liaising with other departments and reaching a figure for the number and type of seats required for the next season. Seats can be bought on either charter or scheduled flights. Charter seats are bought outright, i.e. cannot be returned if they are not sold. With scheduled seats there is a release period so the initial decision to buy is not quite so set in stone.

With a plan of how many seats are needed for each **gateway**, the manager goes to the airlines and negotiates. This may be in the UK or abroad if the **carriers** are foreign, but this is all the travelling anyone in the department is going to do: it's a desk job. There are very few aviation managers; it's a high-level job for experienced personnel who tend to know each other and their buying contacts from their years in the industry.

The manager may negotiate an entire planeful of seats, perhaps at a new time of day not currently being run by that airline. Or, if only a few seats are needed, the manager might negotiate to buy some from another tour operator who doesn't need the capacity.

Karin Frisch works for the Panorama Holiday Group as their aviation planner. She says: 'My manager goes out to negotiate the **contracted flying** and brings the contracts back to us, then they're input into the system so that the information is distributed. Scheduled is contracted at the same time as charter, possibly a little later on. Scheduled is more expensive but some people want a better flight, or they might want to fly on different days or have a long weekend instead of a week. It's very popular.'

Karin has been working in this department for two years and has set up and now runs a planning database, and is responsible for the booking system used by the company.

'I make sure the flights are on sale at the brochure stage and make sure they're all coded correctly,' she says. She has a degree in Travel and Tourism Management from a four-year BA Honours sandwich course. She worked her third (sandwich) year at Panorama, in different sections of the company, and then for longer in Commercial (aviation is a part of the commercial department). The degree was basically a business degree plus a travel module. 'I didn't have a desperate urge to travel,' she explains. 'I just didn't want to do a straight business degree.

'I loved my sandwich year. I learned a lot more in a year here than in the degree. It was a very good insight into the travel industry. I didn't really want to go back to finish my degree. But I did, and after my degree I temped for a while with lots of different companies, then a job came up at Panorama. I did that for a while then I moved sideways into the aviation side. It's interesting. I'm surprised at how much I do already know. I spent time in sales, which was exactly how I expected it to be. Here, I wasn't entirely sure what to expect and it was a pleasant surprise. And it uses aspects of my business skills such as Excel and letter-writing.'

SKILLS YOU'LL NEED
- Good administrative skills.
- Commercial skills for using the systems.
- Excellent planning skills.
- Negotiating skills for the buying process at manager level.
- Not necessarily a degree, but a good grounding in business systems to go in at Karin's level.

PRACTICAL INSIDER INFORMATION ON HOW TO GET THE JOB

'A degree can be a benefit and can be necessary for some jobs, but some companies like it if you have no knowledge of travel so they can train you themselves,' advises Karin. 'It's tough to get work if you want something specific as there are a lot of people out there looking for this sort of work. It's easier to get into the call centre. Repping is another area that gives easier access to working in travel as there are lots of jobs, but it's a tough way in.

'Work experience is very beneficial. The work placement was the best thing ever. I'd have started far lower down the scale without it. Get work experience and try to do everything,' she says. 'Gain as much knowledge as you can in a work experience environment.'

GLOSSARY
- **Carrier**
Transport provider, i.e. airline.
- **Contracted flying**
The seats that are bought in bulk by negotiation early on, rather than the *ad hoc* buying of seats in the 'lates period', which are needed for last-minute sales later in the season.
- **Gateway**
A resort or destination.

Bar Work Overseas

Travelling the world. Wow! Lots of people who need to support themselves en route work the bars (cafés, restaurants, stalls, etc.) at their stopover points. Spend six months, six years, your whole life: it can be addictive.

There's always bar work available if you know what you're doing and go to the right places. It's not usually regulated as formally overseas as in the UK. You might be officially 'employed' but probably you'll just turn up for your shifts and work when you're needed. It can be hard work and conditions can be indifferent: you need to be determined, and work at it. Contacts you make once working will probably get you out of the seedier dives into better places.

You may need a work permit to do this: outside Europe, you certainly will. Many employers don't worry about things like that, but if there's any problem – if, say, you get injured – there'll be no support or comeback. Better to do it formally and legally. Some places you'll earn well enough, and if you can eat (and maybe board) at work, you'll need very little money to live on. The best way to find out is to ask everyone you know where they went and what it was like. The chances are you'll get a few introductions and work will lead on from there.

Annette Matthews spent eight years working in bars in Gibraltar. She didn't mean to – it just kind of happened. 'I always wanted to travel, it was always my huge interest. I left school after GCSEs and worked for a small airline in Plymouth. I was there for two years, then I backpacked around Europe for six months – that was brilliant. I ended up in Gibraltar because I could work there. I worked around the bars for eight years. Gibraltar is a stop-off point for a lot of people: there are lots of yachts on their way to the Caribbean. You get to know people, which I loved. There's a huge expat community. Lots of people travel the world working in bars. They were the main people that I met. Also crews trying to get working passages in Caribbean yachts.'

People like Annette often come back to the UK and work in the travel business here: Annette now works for an airline. Others settle down abroad, perhaps marrying into local families or setting up their own businesses, or just keep travelling. 'I loved it,' says Annette, 'but I didn't want to work in bars for the rest of my life; I wanted to do more.'

It's not always travel that people are after: getting away from the stresses of modern grey-sky living is an ambition for some. Carla Richards bought the **concession** for the pool bar in a privately owned complex of 85 apartments in Lanzarote. 'I was working out here as a rep and decided to stay. The man who used to run this had had enough so I bought it off him two years ago.' She enjoys the life: a gentle pace of work in an informal setting in the sun. But there are drawbacks: 'It's good when the complex is full but when it's low season I just want to pack up and do my own stuff. But I can't, because the apartment owner has contracts with the tour operators and their brochures say there's a poolside bar, so I have to be open all the times stated in my contract, which I hadn't thought about before I started.

'It's a good living, and fun when it's busy, but it's hard work. The last thing I want to do when it's hot is fry chips, but that's what people want so I do it. I get to choose the music, though. I like my customers; most of them are friendly and want to chat. It's the low season that's difficult. I still make just about enough to live on because the

cost of living's low out here, but I won't get rich on it and I won't want to do it for ever. But I don't want to go back to the UK. When I've had enough of this I'll find something else out here. It's a good lifestyle; there's no real pressure, not like at home.'

Annette's advice is not to run your own bar when you're young as you'll get stuck there, but it depends what you're after. And maybe you won't know until you've done it. As Carla says: 'Lots of people want to work out here because of the weather and the way of life. It's much healthier. But most people go back after their holidays and forget about it. Only a few come out here permanently.'

And Annette agrees: 'It's a very easy life running a bar in Spain or Gibraltar, if you like that sort of life.'

Caution: there are many dangers in casual travel and work, especially if you are alone. Get a decent book on working your way around the world and heed its advice.

SKILLS YOU'LL NEED

● You need to like a string of continually changing people and genuinely want to chat to them, listen and socialise.

● Be prepared to work hard when it's busy; to be happy for your customers to be on holiday while you're working.

● Be happy with antisocial hours.

● Some experience of bar work, waiting and other skills is useful if you work in a café or restaurant. If you're planning to buy into a business you need to research what this really means and have some knowledge of running a business. For information on self-employment talk to your local Enterprise Agency – go to them with an outline of the business you plan to set up and they should let you in to their subsidised business seminars.

● You'll need to know the law and business practices of the country you're in, as well as the visa and work requirements; or at least, know where to find out. Do your research well before you commit yourself to anything. Take legal advice.

GLOSSARY
● **Concession**
The right to run a business as your own. In this situation it means buying the business as a going concern, but not actually owning the main business or the land.

BLUE BADGE GUIDE

TRAVEL 6/10, but only in the UK. You might also find work as a tour manager in Europe – see separate chapter.

MONEY: £125 a day plus tips for tours in English in London; a little more if you are guiding in another language. You can develop contacts giving work with high tips, but you can't rely on it. You probably won't work full-time.

HOURS: Irregular work but usually standard half- or full days.

HEALTH RISK: 4/10. Burn-out after a few years if you work too much, but most guides pace themselves and, with a variety of work, it's a healthy existence.

PRESSURE RATING: 4–8/10. Depends hugely on the clients and where you are taking them; can be a gentle, happy day, can be a nightmare of foreign teenagers going AWOL.

GLAMOUR RATING: 5/10. Respected, in control, followed everywhere … But you travel in a coach and, sadly, rarely drink champagne or mix with celebs.

Blue Badge guides are registered through the UK tourist boards and provide guiding services, mostly to foreign visitors, but also to groups travelling within the UK. Most venues and reputable tour companies and agencies ask for the Blue Badge qualification for the guides they employ.

As a guide you travel with a group of tourists explaining anything and everything about the sites visited. You'll guide them through the intricacies of the British system: our culture, history, geography, etiquette, monarchy, toilets and telephones. Whatever they want to know, you tell them. For half a day or a week or two (as a tour manager), you devote yourself to their education and pleasure.

Linda qualified as a London Blue Badge guide three years ago and has been working part-time, and full-time in summer, since. She guides London panoramic tours where, for either a full or half day, she shows visitors the highlights of the city. She tailors these tours according to the group and their special requests, although the itinerary will already have been fixed by the tour company.

She meets the group at their hotel, typically at 9 a.m. for a morning tour. 'They can be anything in number from a large Malaysian family to a group of fifty. There's a huge variety of visitors: you have to be flexible and be prepared. You can't tell the same things to fifty American teenagers as you can to fifty ladies of the Women's Institute.' Linda doesn't wear the same type of clothes for every job, either; she is always smartly dressed but will wear what she feels will fit best with the group she is guiding.

'I chat on the microphone all the time when I'm guiding, even in traffic jams. The Blue Badge course is very good in preparing you for this: what to say, when to say it, how to deal with new places, how to bluff your way through if you really are caught unawares. Your throat gets dry by the end, but again, the course teaches you how to project and protect your voice.'

After various stops for photographs, or perhaps a pre-booked tour of St Paul's Cathedral or a similar hot spot, the tour typically ends with the Changing of the Guard at Buckingham Palace. Linda keeps her group together in the huge crowd before shepherding them back on to the coach, probably leaving them in the centre of London so that they continue with another tour. She then either starts again, or goes home. This panoramic tour is the bread-and-butter work for most London guides. 'I enjoy it. But I can do it blindfold so it's nice to mix it with other tours.'

When she is asked to undertake a new tour, Linda researches the material in her own time. 'You're thrown in completely at the deep end,' she says. 'I'll do Tate Modern soon, accompanying a group of middle-aged ladies. That'll be quite a challenge. I'll visit a few times first, do my research and work out a tour route. We were taught how to do this on the course, as well as how to make associations in the visitors' minds with other places they have visited. It's nerve-racking the first few times you do a new tour, but I enjoy it.'

Linda made contact early on with a company organising tours for British organisations, and she accompanies groups of more mature British people on trips of specific interest to them. She found this contact through a party arranged to allow new guides and tour operators to meet: 'Tour operators like to employ the new guides; they like to try them out. I chatted to several people at the party and got on especially well with this particular woman, who has given me a lot of work.' Ninety per cent of this work is with British people, but this is rare.

'It's fun,' says Linda of her work. 'I enjoy it, mostly, though it's not something I want to do for ever: I want to develop another career. If you do the panoramic tour of London morning and afternoon all week, then it can get a bit tedious. People mostly fall into this. Some do it all their lives but a lot of people move on. But once you're qualified, you're always a Blue Badge guide and you can use it as a sideline or fall back on it. It's a lovely second career. If you're office-based, for instance, it gets you in touch with people and gets you out.'

WORKING PATTERNS

There's little financial security, which is spelled out when you apply for the course, but as Linda says: 'It doesn't always sink in then.' Some people do guiding as a hobby or to subsidise another type of work, and unless you have a niche area for your guiding that keeps you in demand, you essentially have to take whatever work is offered to you.

A lot of actors and teachers do guiding work when they are 'resting' or between academic terms. The peak season is March to October; there's not much work in the winter months and you'll need good contacts to keep working, as there is plenty of competition. There is increased demand for certain languages in certain months, such as Italian when most Italians visit in August.

LANGUAGES

There are already plenty of Blue Badge guides who guide only in English. These guides work mainly with American and Malaysian visitors. Trainees are normally now required to have an additional language (though ask for current requirements). When Linda qualified there was a huge demand for Russian-speaking guides; since then, demand has dropped owing to the Russian domestic situation. The same could apply to other languages and nationalities. Clearly, people from those countries with wealthier citizens, a good economy and a greater travel culture are more likely to visit the UK, and those are the languages you need. The more languages you have, the better your chance of staying in work. 'A couple of European languages and a nice exotic one,' as Linda puts it, would be good. You need to be extremely proficient, either having the language to degree level or having lived in the country in question for a number of years. Many Blue Badge guides speak additional languages that they are not fluent enough to qualify to guide in. There is an oral language test before you are accepted on a course.

QUALIFYING

You have to pay the cost of your training, which will be around £2,500 for the fees, books, fees for exams and the research you'll have to do (London prices). Some courses are part-time

over two years, but most areas run intensive six-month courses. You may have to wait for a new course, as some regions only run them every few years. They usually start in October with applications required by early June.

The short course comprises evening and Saturday lectures and plenty of individual study – learning the streets of the city you are qualifying for as well as visiting the tourist attractions and absorbing as much as possible about them. It really is intensive, and it's not possible to continue to work at the same time. Linda says: 'I did enjoy it. A lot of people found it very demanding in terms of the time you have to devote and the knowledge you have to acquire. It depends on what base you go from: if you have worked as a tour manager then you already have a lot of it, such as a very good knowledge of the streets of London.

'I came to London nine months before applying for the course, and walked London a lot, went to museums and picked up knowledge: the more you have prior to the pre-entrance exam, the better.' Linda learned all there is to know about London's attractions, plus those within striking distance, such as Bath and Stratford-upon-Avon.

The two-year course is less intensive, with tuition from October to April, assessment, and then the summers free. Both versions of the course cover aspects of British history and culture, practical training in guiding skills, site visits, and so on. The course is very tough though once on, most people complete it successfully, some with an exam re-sit, maybe several.

OTHER GUIDING WORK

Many people work as guides at cultural attractions, and are recruited and trained locally. The work is often seasonal, and advertised in JobCentres and the local press. Often a language is needed, so advertisements may also appear at language schools and in the language departments of universities. No qualification is needed beyond the same fluency, usually in one European language, as the Blue Badge guide needs. The same personal skills are required.

SKILLS YOU'LL NEED

● Almost certainly at least one additional language, spoken fluently.
● A reasonable amount of prior background knowledge to get you through the pre-entrance exam.
● You need to be
– flexible so that you can present information in a variety of different ways to entertain and inform any type of group.
– quite outgoing.
– smart, and able to tailor your image to a particular group.
– patient: people ask very silly questions, or ask questions that you have already answered several times when they weren't listening.
● You must like being around people: it's not for people with a short fuse.
● You need a good memory and sense of direction.
● You don't need academic qualifications, though Linda estimates

that three-quarters of guides probably have degrees.
● You can be aged anything from 20 to 60.
● You need to be prepared to arrange your life around your work, and to work weekends and holiday times.

'But the main thing,' says Linda, 'is to have a second career, or else enough languages to keep you in work all the time. There are too many guides out there, really.'

PRACTICAL INSIDER INFORMATION ON HOW TO GET THE JOB

Get to know your area really well before you apply: you won't get a place on the course without a certain amount of local knowledge, and the more time you have to learn the streets of your city, the better. Network with the tour operators at the end-of-course get-together and at any other opportunity. If you work as a tour manager or in another role in a tour company first, these contacts will help. Otherwise, call the agencies and ask to go on their books, and send your CV around. When there is demand some of them will probably try you out, as the qualification is prestigious and they know you will be good. Some specialise: if you have a specialist subject area, this can help. Your local tourist board can supply the names and contact details for tour companies as well as agencies.

USEFUL ADDRESSES

These two associations both administer Blue Badge guiding: it doesn't matter which one you belong to. Both will send you information on becoming a guide.

● Association of Professional Tourist Guides, 40 Bermondsey Street, London SE1 3UD. Tel: 020 7403 2962. www.touristguides.org.uk

For training, they will refer you to: Guide Training (London), 33 Greencroft Gardens, London NW6 3LN. Fax: 020 7625 9693 (no phone contact).

● Guild of Registered Tourist Guides, 52D Borough High Street, London SE1 1XN. Tel: 020 7403 1115. guild@blue-badge.org.uk, www.blue-badge.org.uk/guild

For areas outside London, contact your local tourist board for information: addresses are in Appendix 1.

BROCHURE PRODUCTION

Brochure production is a creative and design side of the travel business that doesn't employ many people in the UK but can be a good career for people interested in travel who are looking to make it in art and design. The larger tour operators have their own in-house studios where brochures are put together. Smaller tour operators contract the work out to specialist brochure design and production companies.

Although each individual case is different, the Panorama Holiday Group brochure studio is a good example of how it works: 'Our studio is based on PCs, rather than Apple Macs, and we have seven people involved in brochure production,' says Martin Young, Sales and Marketing Director. 'We create everything in-house, up to the repro stage. Then we output it to a repro house on a disk, then it goes on to the printers.'

The team creates the images we will see in the brochure. 'We design it all in-house,' says Martin. 'We moved away from outside studios because of the cost, and to regain control.' The process starts with bringing together information, including photographs, from overseas about the **product**. These are either supplied by agencies, taken by members of the Panorama staff, or by a freelance photographer sent out by Martin. The studio assembles the overseas content along with factual information from the contracting department. The commercial department fills in pricing information and any tactical offers, such as how many in a group booking will travel free of charge. This information is input by **artworkers** into the machines and the end result is the brochure that sells the holidays.

Studio managers are in charge; they design the templates for the brochure then co-ordinate its production. Different people work on different sections of each brochure. For instance, if it's a brochure of 160 pages, there isn't time for it to be produced by just one artworker. The manager ensures that the overall look is right and that the content is accurate, buys print, meets deadlines, and so on. It's a thinking-ahead role, ensuring that each brochure in production is ready and meeting deadlines, and planning the next ones. The manager will probably have started as an artworker and risen to manager after a number of years' experience.

'The whole brochure production function is going to spin off into the new media,' says Martin. The Panorama studio already repackages the same information into different formats for other media: 'We give the TV Travel Shop a slightly repackaged product,' he says. 'It won't be in the brochure, and it'll be repriced. They often need a film crew to go and film: we get our people in resort to assist the crew that goes out.'

COPYWRITING AND OTHER ROLES

Panorama doesn't have enough work to employ a full-time copywriter. 'We usually go to a professional copywriter for the basic text for a new destination,' explains Martin. 'If it's just bits and pieces, the team will get involved.'

They also use the department as an in-house production resource for promotional items such as **point-of-sale leaflets**. This gives everyone a more varied job content. 'This department is quite stylish,' says Martin, 'more than some other departments, so it requires a creative frame of mind.'

SKILLS YOU'LL NEED

It's a production function with an element of design, so you need to be creative, with an art school and formal design background. The work is similar to magazine production processes, so useful research would be to find out more about the publishing industry. People come from all sorts of backgrounds after their education. It takes very organised people who are able to assemble and deal with large amounts of information. Artworkers need some keyboard experience.

PRACTICAL INSIDER INFORMATION ON HOW TO GET THE JOB

'We welcome people with other aptitudes, for instance an art person to work on the keyboards. Some companies don't, as it's more tightly structured.' Artworkers sometimes come through design agencies. Otherwise, write around and see what vacancies exist.

GLOSSARY
● **Artworker**
The artworker fulfils the basic role: inputs the keyboards, squeezes pictures of hotels on to the page. It's a data-entry-plus role.
● **Point-of-sale leaflets**
Leaflets available to the public at the place where the sales are made, such as beside a till or on a travel agent's desk.
● **Product**
The thing that's being sold, in this case a package holiday.

BUSINESS TRAVEL CONSULTANT

TRAVEL RATING: 3/10. You'll be office-based but go on 'educationals', trips to increase your knowledge of transport and destinations. If you're good, you may win enough educationals to see the world.

MONEY: Very good for the travel biz. Trainee salaries start at about £11,000–12,000. You might earn £20,000-plus after four or five years' experience in business travel. Part of this is commission.

HOURS: Office hours but there may be some shift work.

HEALTH RISK: 2/10. Unless a filing cabinet falls on your head you should be fine.

PRESSURE RATING: 6/10. It's intensive work, much of it on the telephone or computer, and mistakes can be costly. For some people that's fun; for others it's stressful.

GLAMOUR RATING: 4/10. It pays well, and there's a certain glamour within the industry. But the actual work, to an outsider, might not seem glam at all.

Businesspeople who travel for their work often do so separately from holidaymakers: they travel in different parts of the plane or train, drink more champagne and have their own travel agents to arrange this for them. These agents, or consultants, deal with all aspects of businesspeople's travel needs.

Business travel is big business: one traveller may spend as much on a short journey as a whole family can spend on its annual holiday. The work is similar to leisure travel agency work (see the Travel Agent section). It involves talking with your client on the phone or face to face and buying travel products to suit their requirements. This might be a simple flight ticket, or could involve planning an entire **itinerary** for them, including advising on the best airline and flight timings, the most suitable location for a hotel, and then the best hotel on offer.

You'll have a file for each client detailing their travel, dietary and other requirements, which you'll call up on to your screen whenever you do some work for that person. You'll also have the latest in booking and research technology at your fingertips. You'll need this, because your job is to arrange the most reliable, cost-effective and comfortable way of travelling to ensure that the client arrives at their destination on time. This involves more than just flights and accommodation: often ground arrangements need to be made, such as car or limousine hire.

Jenny is an experienced travel consultant with a small agency. She explains how it works: 'We have a large number of small business client companies, rather than working for just a few huge companies, which the larger agencies do. When one of our clients needs to travel, they phone us, and their regular contact takes the call.'

Jenny explains that it's important to develop a business relationship with each client, so that they will have confidence in you and your work. 'As soon as my client calls, I call their file up on my screen and scan it for their most recent trips and their usual requirements. Then I ask them their plans.'

The client explains the trip, with the necessary timings, and Jenny keys these in and sets to work trying to fulfil those needs. 'It can take lots of time on the computer and telephone,' she says. 'Sometimes it's very last-minute and you have to try to find the last ticket on a flight. Or all the hotels you try are already full because your client is making a last-minute dash to a conference where the whole city is booked up.'

Once she's found the best seats and rooms she will usually check back with the client, though sometimes she'll book straight away depending on her client's instructions. Sometimes there are last-minute changes of plan. 'You can spend hours working out an itinerary then check back and find that the whole trip is off,' she says. 'Or tickets you've booked may have to be changed, often several times, because of changes to meetings and other arrangements. It happens all the time. You just have to smile and look forward to their next call.'

Jenny also advises on visa and currency requirements, and some travel consultants will also arrange these.

DIFFERENT WORKPLACES

There are two types of locations where you can work: implants and outplants. Implants are areas within the client's office where you and your colleagues set up a mini travel agency, arranging only that client's travel needs. Here you'll have much more face-to-face contact with your clients. In an outplant you'll work in your employer's offices, which may be some distance from the client. You may never get to meet them, though your employer could arrange visits or special events so that you can meet up and foster the business relationship you are developing.

WHAT'S IT LIKE

'I love it,' says Jenny. 'It's very varied, though I know it doesn't sound like it. I love making really complicated itineraries, and getting them right so that if a client asks me to check something they feel might be wrong, it isn't: I've always got it spot on.' Another insider disagrees: 'It's very boring. It's sitting in front of your desk with a headset and a computer saying "Can I help you?" and tapping in information, then asking them to make their choice from what comes up. The core job isn't much different to retail: you tap in, then relay the information, then they choose. The difference is that you're dealing with corporate clients. You're also mostly on the phone rather than face to face, unless you're working in an implant.'

As you progress, you'll take on more responsibility. Later, you might move on to field sales, preparing and delivering the tenders for new accounts, or rise to implant or divisional manager.

SKILLS YOU'LL NEED

You need an interest and knowledge of geography, good basic GCSEs including maths and English (though these aren't vital), a confident, pleasant and tenacious personality, be able to work alone or as part of a team, be very strong on detail, checking your facts all the time, and very determined: you need to be a puzzle-solver. You also need to be able to do all this under pressure, and keep smiling (yes, even down the phone).

Before you enter business travel or during your training, you need to gain your **BA Fares and Ticketing 1&2** (one of several International Air Transport Association (IATA)-approved ticketing courses – see Appendix 3 for more details), or equivalent, plus knowledge of a **Central Reservations System (CRS)**.

Your clients will all speak English, as will the vast majority of the travel organisations you deal with, so a language is not necessary.

PRACTICAL INSIDER INFORMATION ON HOW TO GET THE JOB

Some of the larger business travel consultancies offer training schemes for college leavers who have completed CRS training and fares & ticketing qualifications. 'The multiple business travel companies offer first-class in-house training courses to college leavers and graduates wishing to enter this field,' says a recruiter. She recommends that you write to the human resources departments of the larger agencies and ask about their graduate training schemes.

Many business travel consultants are experienced retail travel agents who make the sideways move into business travel, or they may have come from long-haul tour operators, consolidators and airlines. 'Travel companies ideally like candidates who have a well-rounded knowledge of airline routings and fares,' says a recruiter, 'who have first-hand knowledge of making reservations on one of the major computer systems such as Sabre, Galileo or Amadeus and who have the necessary customer service skills to deal with the varying demands of today's busy corporate traveller. And it's not only young people who join the travel industry. Just as many mature candidates join.'

GLOSSARY

● **BA Fares and Ticketing 1&2**
This is probably the most prestigious ticketing qualification, but there are others that are equally good, such as the Air France or Lufthansa qualifications. They each carry the necessary ten International Air Transport Association (IATA) points, which means that they have had to cover certain criteria on the course.

● **Central Reservations Systems (CRS)**
These are computer systems allowing you to access the booking processes of airlines and other travel organisations. There are four systems; the two most popular currently are Sabre and Galileo Focalpoint. The differences are like the differences between learning Microsoft Word for Windows or Wordperfect.

● **Itinerary**
A detailed plan of a route, with timings and often instructions.

CALL CENTRE STAFF

TRAVEL RATING: 3/10. You may go on **educationals**. Otherwise it's an office job.

MONEY: Low basic (from £7,000), but if you're good you can earn well with the right employer. Part of your pay is **commission** on items you sell.

HOURS: General office hours or shift work.

HEALTH RISK: 8/10. It's burn-out: people do it for a couple of years at the most, but some move into management or other roles in travel.

PRESSURE RATING: 8/10. All sales is pressured. Telesales, staring at a screen, is more so for most people.

GLAMOUR RATING: 0/10. Headset. Screen. Disembodied voices. Not most people's first choice.

Call centres are the places you phone when you want to book a holiday, flight or other travel product direct with a tour operator or carrier, or via an agency such as a television channel, website or text service.

They have a bad reputation all round. For consumers, it can take ages to get through and once you do you may be kept holding on, and then may get talked at by a member of staff whose income level depends on you booking that product, and who may not know very much about it. From an employee's point of view they have gained a reputation for being 'the new workhouses' – hard, exhausting and dull work, bad conditions and poor treatment by management.

So why do they exist? Travel is a very, very competitive industry, and all the players are doing their utmost to get the business. They have worked out that an office (or a warehouse) full of motivated and even aggressive salespeople offering good deals to a bargain-hungry public can 'up' their sales and lower the amount they pay in commission to travel agents. They seem to be right: despite the poor service from some (not all) call centres, the public appears to keep phoning, sometimes shunning the services of their local travel agent, who, in many cases, can get them an equally good deal.

But, hey! It's not all doom and gloom: the headlines highlight the largest and newsworthiest of the call centres, but there are many organisations that run what are essentially renamed reservations departments, where the staff are long-term and well trained, work in good conditions and understand their product. Here, working in the call centre can be the beginning of a career in travel or, if not, in any sales or service-based occupation. It's excellent training: if you are good at this, you have a skill that you'll use for ever.

Why else do it? The pay can look appealing, if you believe the commission rates they quote (which if you're good, can be as high as they state); the people who recruit you are salespeople themselves so know how to lure you in; the atmosphere can be very exciting if it's a well-managed team; you'll probably be working with like-minded and similarly aged people; you'll move up the ranks very fast if it suits you, and you have to start somewhere. Oh yes, and they're always recruiting. Staff turnover rates are high, as they are for any sales work, so for as long as call centres continue to flourish there'll be vacancies. If it's the right thing for you and you have the appropriate skills it's one of the few 'easy' ways into the travel industry ('easy' meaning there are plenty of jobs, not meaning that they hand these out to just anyone).

THE ENVIRONMENT

'Some call centres are like a conveyor belt and they are literally processing bookings; the consultants can't even go to the toilet without permission. Our call centre deals as much with administrative queries: it's a customer service provider as well.' So says David West of Panorama. 'They can be fun, exciting places to work,' adds Dean Robinson, one of Panorama's call centre team leaders. 'At one travel company,' he says, 'they have a round table and screens for noise blocking, but can you imagine sitting there for seven hours a day with a computer screen and a telephone? In our call centre you can look over and see everyone and people walking past. It does get noisy sometimes, but that's better than not seeing anyone all day. Another call centre is in a warehouse where they have about five hundred consultants. To make it nicer for them

they have a waterfall running through and flashing lights coming up from the floor, a big fountain and coloured animals on the walls.'

Whatever the décor (and you'll see this when you are shown around at interview: don't take the job if they won't show you where you'll be working!), your desk or cubicle will contain a computer screen and keyboard, a headset and telephone, and the brochures and other literature you'll need, plus the usual odds and ends. You could be working in communication with other members of your team – perhaps to reach team targets together, and to be able to ask colleagues questions about the product if you don't have access to the information yourself – or you might find that there is little contact with other people and that you work alone with a manager's support and the customer on the other end of the telephone line.

THE WORK

The job is taking incoming telephone calls (possibly eighty or more a day) and converting these into sales. There may also be an element of calling customers or agents back with information that you had to go and research. Some organisations may also ask that you spend slack time calling customers or travel agents '**cold**' and promoting your product.

Call centre management varies hugely. With some of the newer and faster-expanding centres staff turnover is so high that employees don't always have the necessary background that will enable them to do the work effectively, and there isn't always enough training. Hayley Williams is an experienced travel agency consultant who started working for one such call centre, a new and rapidly growing agency selling cheap package holidays from many different tour operators. 'I only stayed for six months because it made me feel like a robot. Anyone could do it: you didn't need any travel agency experience. At first they only took people with travel experience, but then it grew so fast they took other people, and there were so many mistakes then. It wasn't for me. I like to take time with my customers and get to know them.'

Jane Barter describes the scale of the call centre she worked for as a manager: 'It was amazing how much business came through those phones twenty-four hours a day, with people queuing. Some of the deals were excellent, but some you could get in a travel agent.' Jane found it very stressful as a manager, and feels that it was stressful for the sales consultants, too. 'You can't spend an hour on the phone talking to the customer if you've got calls waiting,' she explains. 'Two minutes on the phone feels like a long time. Yet you don't want to get rid of a customer because you want to give a good service. It was very stressful running around saying we've got ten calls waiting, can you wind it up. They were still encouraged to try to build up that customer rapport; it was just the pressure. It's either going to be for somebody or it isn't. We'd have a big turnover and then suddenly people would stay for a long time, and then they'd have enough and want to move

on.' Jane understands that some people thrive in that environment but, she says: 'It just wasn't me. I like to talk to customers and see their reactions. It was a totally different ballgame and didn't suit what I was looking for.'

Call centres are a new part of the industry and are still finding their feet. While some are huge and have probably outgrown a comfortable size for the workers, others maintain a personal touch and a strong connection with the travel industry, which sometimes seems lost in the frenetic activity of the warehouses. Panorama's is an example of a smaller, home-grown call centre. Dean Robinson explains how it works: 'Our call centre consultants get incoming calls. About ninety per cent are from travel agents and the rest are from direct clients. You can tell as soon as you pick up the call where they are from, and you do relate to travel agents differently than you do to clients. You get to know some of them, too: when you take travel agents on educationals and meet them face to face, then they phone and ask for you when they've got a booking. We don't call agents cold with special offers as we used to when we were a smaller company. Now we're so busy we haven't got time to do it.

'Most people in the call centre are aged seventeen to twenty-three, apart from part-time people. It is a young person's place; it's happy and lively, very social too. You go to lunch together and out in the evenings. We have had older people who have fitted in but you can see there is a bond between the younger people.

'We try to take eleven to twelve calls per consultant per hour, about seventy to eighty calls a day. Calls last from a couple of minutes checking a phone number to a good hour.'

David West continues: 'Travel agents do ninety per cent of their bookings on **viewdata** but they might want more detailed information, and phone in.' Panorama has built a system of information files to enable anyone in the call centre to answer any question on anything – or almost anything: 'Our databank includes the directors, as we are still a small enough company. If the call centre people really can't find an answer they might ask us, so then they can close the sale.' Although Panorama's consultants are trained to sell, because most of the calls they get are dealing with agents who will close the deal with the customer, it's not a hard sell.

But wherever you work, it is essentially a sales job. Dean describes how even at the relatively soft-sell Panorama call centre 'the people we employ now are more sales-focused. They do get a buzz out of it. If someone phones up to book Tunisia but Tunisia is full and you sell them Morocco you think: I've done that. And you really hope that person likes that holiday, and you want to speak to them when they come back and see if they had a good time.'

Sales is the backbone of any commercial organisation. 'It is the hub of the business,' says David West, 'and it sets the tone for the environment that we work in. When the call centre's quiet then business is slow, when it's busy everyone's busy; there's a knock-on effect that affects the atmosphere in the building. In January, February and March everyone is hyped up because it's the peak booking time. We try to create an environment where the call centre doesn't get disturbed and everyone supports them. It's important that the agents get through very quickly.'

STRESSES AND STRAINS

David explains how the strain builds up over time. 'We put in place a two-year contract for call centre staff,' he says, 'because after two years they're either exceptional, or they need to move on. Constantly being on the phone gets so you want to scream, and a lot of it is answering the same questions. We've been lucky that in the last few years we have been growing and people have been able to move into other areas.' Dean agrees: 'After about a year it gets very tedious: think about answering the phone from nine to five thirty and reading the same information from the same brochures.'

INCENTIVES

When you need intelligent, personable people to do a job which, everyone agrees, gets a little wearing after a while, they need incentives. Call centre staff, like all salespeople, work at least partly on a commission basis.

'Staff are monitored throughout the year on their target performance, call monitoring, attendance record and product knowledge,' says Dean. 'They have a target set every month, to book, say, three hundred heads. If they do this they get an increase in salary at the end of the year. The average commission is £200 a month and the maximum commission one of the consultants earned in January, our busiest month, was £520.

'They get incentives nearly every day: the person who answers the most telephone calls today wins a bottle of wine, and so on. We also have a nominations system: if someone helps you out, you nominate them, and the person with the most nominations gets to choose an envelope with a prize in it. Incentives are a big part of call centres all the time. In sales, if we said there were no incentives and someone phoned in to book a holiday, they would just talk; if they're going to earn five pounds they are really going to sell it.'

TRAVELLING

Travel is also an incentive. Many call centres offer 'prizes' of educational visits to resorts for the highest-achieving consultants. But as well as that, good call centres want staff to understand the product they are selling and will send them out to discover for themselves what it's like. Specialist tour operator Neilson sells through the trade and direct to the public. Joe Lynch explains: 'Because we offer a bit more than the standard holiday we have reservations staff specially trained to talk about the sailing and activities and individual resorts. They go out to see them so they can give first-hand knowledge, which is an important part of their work.'

It's in the Panorama staff contracts that staff go overseas on educationals

twice a year. Dean has been to fifteen countries in three years, though this is not the norm. David West explains the rationale: 'We used to use educationals as the main product training tool but now they're used more as a motivational tool, as the product has become so big. Staff will go to two resorts in a year, with a minimum of four days on most trips.' One call centre consultant said: 'When you've been there you can tell the client much more than is in the brochure, which they can read for themselves anyway. You can tell them all about it. It's much better.'

TRAINING

Travel industry call centres prefer staff experienced in travel work, whether repping in resort, selling in a high-street travel agency, or something else. Then they'll already have some idea of how the business works and be able to talk expertly about at least some destinations. In reality, with the low starting salary and the continuing demand for consultants, many people are new to travel when they start in a call centre. Training is therefore vital, both in how to sell, and product knowledge.

At Panorama's call centre, staff are trained on the job during their probationary three months and then go on several sales skills courses over the following couple of months. The courses cover sales techniques such as open and closed questions, tone of voice, building rapport with clients, and so on, all of which are important in the work. After another six months they go on an advanced sales skills course. At the same time, on-the-job training continues. 'It's half and half really,' says Dean, who trains five staff. 'You put it together and it all works.' This training includes call monitoring: 'I listen in to their calls some days. I listen for whether they build a rapport with their clients; if a travel agent asks how far it is to the beach, what they say if they don't know; their response time; also how long they leave the phone if it's ringing. We have a call monitoring form with different levels and we total them at the end. If they get eighty per cent they pass. If they don't, we go over it and look at the areas they need to improve then discuss it again the next month.'

Dean also conducts three-month reviews with his staff: these are chats to make sure everything is going well. He sets them objectives such as sales targets, or to redevelop a filing system, or try to promote a certain product by calling a few travel agents, and so on. He also asks them if they want to develop and what they want to do next.

CAREER PROGRESSION

'It's a very good way into travel because we are not looking for loads of qualifications,' says David West. 'If there's a good internal policy within the company then you can move on to other areas, or apply externally.' Dean agrees: 'It is often the first step for people, like it was for me. Some people have gone on to administration, to overseas, or to other call centres. And while a lot of people go repping then come here, some people do it the other way around. The maximum lifespan is

about a year, or a year and a half. A lot of people go on to the commercial department, where you're loading flights and bedrooms into the system for the call centre to sell. I sometimes think: you've come from the sales area and been on the phone talking to people, and gone to this? But people used to want to get out of the call centre; I think now it's changing because the call centre is becoming more exciting and there is more opportunity to earn money.'

Jane Barter recalls her time in call centre management: 'I'd had enough of being a manager in a travel agency. I applied for a job at a call centre that was a brand-new initiative, a really good idea. I just wanted a change. It had been going for about nine months when I went to them as a duty manager, looking after ten supervisors with another duty manager. The supervisors had eighteen to twenty-two people each within their teams; that was a really big change. I was doing the rotas for them: sickness, coaching, developing. It was totally different there: it really wasn't for me. But I did know someone who was a travel agent, who went into a call centre as a sales consultant and works in the commercial department now – she moved sideways. The commercial department do all the agreements and the discounts, make sure the staff know about them, and deal with the tour operators to see what deals they can get.'

Jane left fairly soon to manage a Holiday Hypermarket store, but others stay and, as in any sales structure, if it's the right thing for you, you can rise fast. Dean says of his three years in travel: 'If you join a call centre, don't give up. Go on, be enthusiastic and show you can sell. Three years down the line I've been to fifteen countries; I'm earning a good wage and I've made a lot of friends. Call centres are fun, exciting places to work.'

SKILLS YOU'LL NEED

You'll probably be young, partly because everyone else is and partly because the pay won't support your kids. Dean describes a typical call centre consultant:

● They are bubbly people who are not afraid to talk to people. If you're shy you'll find it hard to express yourself.

● Lively and outgoing.

● If you've been to a certain country and are talking to someone who has never been on holiday before, you need to run it through from scratch. You have to be quick-minded, be confident in answering their questions or say: 'I'm sorry, I don't know that but I'll find out for you.'

● Patient: you repeat yourself time and time again. Or else, they're looking at the pictures and they ask the same question and you think to yourself: were they listening at all? But you can't say that.

● You need an eye for detail.

● You don't need to be excellent at maths because you have a calculator and a computer. But you have to focus on what you're doing and how much things are, and work it out on paper. You can't always rely on the computer because if it's been loaded on to the computer wrongly you'll look stupid: you need to check it.

PRACTICAL INSIDER INFORMATION ON HOW TO GET THE JOB

Call centres often need people, but that doesn't mean they'll take just anybody. As Dean says: 'It's quite a tough area to get into and we don't want to waste our time or theirs getting the wrong people, just because we need people.'

When Panorama need a number of staff they run group interviews. This is common practice. Recruiters are looking for 'how they get on with other people', says Dean. 'Some people want to be in front of everyone else and are overpowering, and that wouldn't be any good with a client or in the call centre. You have to get a person with enthusiasm who's not too loud and not too shy. It's quite difficult to find people like that.' Group interviews indicate how you relate to new people, and recruiters devise various ways to test this. For more details of group interviews see the Holiday Representative section.

As it's a telephone job you're applying for, expect to speak on the phone. Panorama follow up the group interview session with a one-to-one interview, at the start of which candidates are told that the telephone will ring at some time during the interview and they are to pick it up. 'There's no right or wrong way of answering it,' says Dean. 'A team leader rings from the call centre and says: "I want to go on holiday." It shows whether they can use their initiative: some of them say: "Hello, this is Panorama Holidays, how can I help you?" They pick up the brochures that are there and use them. You can see straight away if they're a sales person.' Jane Barter agrees. She recruited people to work in the huge call centre she worked at before Holiday Hypermarket: 'Some of the people they took on had no travel experience. We interviewed them in group interviews and they had the personality to sell. In travel it's not necessarily what you know: it's knowing where to find the information. You can tell if someone's going to be a good salesperson.'

'And some people haven't done any research,' says Dean. 'We say: "You've applied for the call centre consultant job," and they look really puzzled! Or you ask what they think the job is about and they just look at you. Others have gone to the travel agent and picked up the brochures or phoned up someone and found out that we are a small family-run company that has sold to Airtours, and really done their homework. That's nice to see.'

GLOSSARY
● **Cold**
Cold calling means contacting someone who hasn't already expressed interest, and selling to them.
● **Commission**
An additional part of your pay on top of your salary. It's never guaranteed, though recruiters might quote 'OTE', On Target Earnings, which is what they would expect you to earn in terms of basic salary plus commission if you settle well into the work. Commission often comes in seasonal lumps (rarely at the times you want it).

● **Educationals**
Trips to resorts so that you can see what the places – and the holidays – are really like.
● **Viewdata**
A system used by travel agents to check availability and to book products for their clients.

CAR HIRE STAFF

*Many travellers need the use of a car,
so car hire offices proliferate around
airports, ports, railway stations, in large
cities and towns. There are thousands
of different car hire businesses, all
competing for the holiday and business
trade. Many of these companies are run
as **franchises** or **agents**; others may be
large organisations which employ
managers and staff for their branches;
and others still are independent
concerns set up by individuals.*

One national car hire chain,
Budget Car and Van Rental,
sold one of its franchises to a
local transport company, and Trevor
McInnes works there as a receptionist,
or rental sales agent. 'The car hire
business looks very simple,' he says.
'But you've got to buy the vehicles,
work out the profit, and then hope that
your customer will take it out and
bring it back in one piece.' If the
customer damages the car then the
insurance company covers most of the
cost of repairs, but the car hire
company will pay the **excess**. This is
rarely recovered in full from the
customer, so it's very important that
receptionists can judge whether a
person is going to look after the
vehicle. 'You need experience for this
work,' says Trevor. 'You decide through
experience whether a person is going
to be a good customer and whether
you're going to rent to someone.
Otherwise you'd just be saying to
everyone who walks in the door:
"Here's a brand-new car. I believe
everything you say: take it."'

Refusing to rent a car to someone
can be embarrassing. Luckily, says
Eddie, who has worked in car rental for
25 years, that has only happened to
him once. 'I recognised a man when
he came in after making a telephone
booking. He had rented a car two years
before and not brought it back.
Luckily, there was something wrong
with his licence so it was easy to refuse
the car.'

Other elements of receptionist
work include using the computer to
locate and book vehicles, logging in

customer details and working out the finances.

You get the experience you need to work as a receptionist by starting as a car cleaner, or service agent. Your job then is to clean and check the vehicles when they are returned to the car hire offices. You'll need to do this work for two years, probably, and gain an understanding of the business and the customers, before progressing to receptionist work.

After this, some people start out in business, either buying a franchise or completely independently. It's a very cut-throat business, says Trevor, and some entrepreneurs fall flat on their faces. Others, though, succeed. One of these is Martin Weller, who set up and runs BVR, a rental company specialising in van as well as car hire. 'I was in the business,' he says, 'and set up on my own six years ago. From the outside it looks very simple, but it's not. Insurance is very hard to get for new car hire businesses, because self-drive hire is the highest-risk insurance on the road. As a new business we started with six second-hand vans. It cost £10,000 to insure these for just third party, fire and theft.' Now he has comprehensive insurance on his fleet of 45 vehicles and things are going well. 'I wouldn't do anything else now,' he says. 'But the first five years were the hardest, with lots of sleepless nights. Now it almost runs itself, and I've got staff to do things like vehicle repairs: I used to do all those myself. You start off with such high outgoings and with old vehicles; people have accidents and the premiums go up. And it's very simple to get too big too

quickly in this game. The way I did it, I bought everything on HP but they were mine. If you lease vehicles they have limited-mileage contracts; the mileage goes up and there are extra charges.'

Car hire is moving towards Internet booking, says Eddie. European or international companies will take a booking either at a local office or through the Internet for car hire abroad. Their offices overseas are usually staffed with nationals of that country, though if your languages are good you could apply for work there.

SKILLS YOU'LL NEED

For any work in car hire you need to be over 21 and hold a full, clean driving licence. For receptionist work you need to have a good understanding of people, probably gained through other customer service work and in your time as a car hire service agent servicing the cars. You also need to deal with customer enquiries by phone, fax or in person, to make reservations through the computer system, handle the paperwork and take payment. These all require general customer service skills as well as organisational ability. 'You need a great deal of patience and tolerance of other people,' says Eddie.

PRACTICAL INSIDER INFORMATION ON HOW TO GET THE JOB

Start by contacting the head offices of the larger car hire companies. Their names are in the Yellow Pages or you can search for them on the Internet. They will tell you their recruitment procedures. Also try local independently owned companies, and franchises which may recruit locally.

You may be able to find work by walking into local offices. 'In twenty-five years I've had people walk in, write, telephone, and come centrally via head office,' says Eddie. 'Though the main way I get people is when they write. I'm looking for a good letter. The ones that impress you most are the ones who write proficiently, and send CVs and photographs, people who show some sort of savvy, more than a little bit of intelligence.'

'Don't go for too big a company,' advises Martin Weller. 'Or all you'll do is make the tea. Go for a smaller set-up where you'll get lots of good experience.' He also advises people thinking of setting up on their own to avoid franchises: 'The actual profit margin is very small,' he says.

GLOSSARY

● Agents
Similar to franchises (see below) but in this instance the parent organisation supplies the vehicles as well, but the agent pays salaries, etc. out of the percentage of takings kept. This percentage is obviously much lower than with a franchise (perhaps 20 per cent of the take to stay with the agent rather than 80 per cent with a franchise).

● Excess
The amount of money you have to pay when something that is insured is stolen or damaged. The insurance company will pay most of the costs but there is always this excess to encourage you to look after the item.

● Franchise
This is a way of running a business. The owner of a large organisation may decide that it is easier, and more profitable, to 'sell' small units of the company to people who want to manage them. The franchisee, who 'buys' the small unit, also buys the use of the company name and logo, insurance for the vehicles, national advertising, computer back-up, and other central expertise. Franchising happens in all sorts of businesses: fast food outlets are often franchises.

CHILDREN'S REPRESENTATIVE

Children's representatives (kiddie reps) look after children from the ages of three up to about twelve or thirteen for certain set periods each day, and perhaps for a couple of evenings each week. Babies use the crèche and are cared for by **nannies**, *but as more and more kiddie reps now have childcare qualifications, reps and nannies have become more interchangeable.*

Many parents choose package holidays because they know their children will be happy and safe in the kids' club for several hours a day. It's an important part of the sales pitch for the tour operators, and they have to get it right. Kids' clubs tend to be large, based in a hotel or apartment complex, well managed and staffed by experienced and often qualified people. As one recruiter puts it: 'We don't want treasure hunts or playing ball or children stuck in a room painting all the time; we try to offer a mix of activities that are more interesting and more in line with what they would get if they went to playgroup or nursery in the UK.'

Janice spent two seasons as a kiddie rep in France with one of the larger camping tour operators: 'I loved it but it was hard work. I've always wanted to work with children, and did some work with smaller kids when I was a teenager. I thought it would be fun to go out to a resort after college, so I went out the summer I graduated. By the end I was so exhausted I vowed I'd never do it again ... but at the same time I'd enjoyed it so much I was prepared to put up with the drawbacks. I spent the winter doing a short childcare course and then last year went out early and helped set up, and got much more involved. It was better that way.'

Although for some people it's the start of a career, for most it's a season or two working in the sun before getting on with other things. Hayley Williams's ambition was to rep before she settled down. She already had experience of working with children as an au pair in the US for a year: 'I went out as a kiddie rep with one of the big tour operators. You have the kids four hours a day, in two sessions, and plan and do different activities. If there weren't so many children to look after we'd take excursions to Barcelona. I really did enjoy all that, and getting to know the families.

'I didn't actually need a qualification before I went; it's like being a playleader. There were seven kiddie reps in one hotel and you were never left on your own, there was always another kiddie rep there. There were four or five reps with up to twenty kids.

'Some parents tried to force their kids into the club but we'd take them back to their parents if they were unhappy. But once they'd met the other kids most of them would never miss another session. We got letters later saying "we miss you".

'There weren't too many hours; it was quite easy compared to repping.' Though she adds: 'Because in some resorts kiddie reps have to do transfers as well, repping is certainly not a holiday. Some days I was working twenty-four hours.'

TRAINING

Although tour operators are careful to vet the people they recruit, and only take those they are sure have good experience and, in some cases, appropriate qualifications, they also invest heavily in training so that they are sure that the reps are up to the work. Hayley spent a long time training before the season started:

'They sent us out to Majorca for a month and we worked in the schools there. Kiddie repping is like working in a class: you have to plan activities, and there are always other staff around. The training was very hard work, seven in the morning until ten at night, and very extensive. You had to pass to get a job. They let a few go at the end of the training.

'Then we flew to resort after the four weeks, and had three weeks' training there. They took us on excursions so that we could lead excursions ourselves. We had on-the-spot training all through the time we were working: at lunch-times, for instance. While I was there I gained my NVQ 2&3 in Children's Representation; the assessors flew out once a month.'

Not all tour companies invest that much time in their reps, but they do have to ensure the safety and wellbeing of the children in their care, so take recruitment and training very seriously.

SKILLS YOU'LL NEED

You won't be considering this work unless you love children. If you think that they are inventively malicious little horrors who boil toads and present them to inexperienced kiddie reps for breakfast, well, you may be right, but it's not the job for you.

More companies are looking for a qualification in childcare: National Nursery Examination Board (NNEB), an NVQ in childcare, or equivalent. For nannies, this is essential. You also need experience of working with children and good references. You will be police-checked. You need to be able to put together a programme of children's activities and think on your feet, work hard and take responsibility.

As well as all this, you need the general skills of repping, such as flexibility, liking all types of people, a good sense of humour, and so on (see Holiday Representative section for more details).

PRACTICAL INSIDER INFORMATION ON HOW TO GET THE JOB

Companies have to be very careful with the people they select, and will make checks on candidates' experience and take up references. Kiddie reps don't usually need a formal childcare qualification, but if you have one you'll find it easier to get the work you want. One recruiter explains how they find their children's reps: 'We have good contacts with the local authorities, and we write to colleges.' You can write direct to tour operators, too. Research this as you would a job as a holiday representative.

At interview, you'll have to show what you can do. 'Children's reps' interviews are done completely differently from other reps,' the recruiter says. 'There are one-to-one interviews with the kids' club controller. It's more probing; they have to come in and make things and put together work plans of how they are going to structure their week. Most have worked in an environment where they can produce a weekly timetable of activities. What we look for are the benefits: what learning are the children going to have? Within nurseries, you have to think about what a child is going to get out of it and we follow on from that. If they've done that training it should be second nature to them.'

GLOSSARY
● **Nanny**
Someone qualified to look after the under-threes. They usually work in the crèche and have a larger child/carer ratio. They may help out with the kids' clubs at times, but kiddie reps can't help out in the crèche without qualifications.

Coach Driver

Travel involves transport and transport involves drivers. Apart from the glam occupation of driving an aircraft (see Pilot section), other ways to steer your career include coach driving.

We have millions of home and incoming tourists and business travellers using our coach and bus services, as well as many UK coach companies taking travellers abroad. All these organisations need drivers. You usually start off on local services, working either for a bus company or a coach company driving for groups such as school day excursions. After that, you'll have the experience to drive longer trips and take groups abroad.

THE WORK

Tour companies taking groups abroad on package holidays always place couriers/managers on vehicles, but companies taking private groups on day trips or longer excursions usually employ just a driver. In this case, you not only drive the coach but also deal with the passengers. Chris Chatfield owns Compass Coaches, a company that provides coaches for private groups. 'There's not normally a courier on board,' says Chris, 'unless it's a larger company, or they're going abroad. So the driver has to get on well with people and give general information.'

As well as driving, you're responsible for keeping the coach clean, loading and unloading luggage, and maintaining the vehicle while on the road. If there's a mechanical fault you will have to arrange repairs, or even find a new vehicle and possibly overnight accommodation for the passengers. This could be difficult in a foreign country.

TRAINING

Before you train and take your PCV (Passenger Carrying Vehicle) licence exam you need to be eighteen or over and hold a full driving licence. From that point, you can join a bus company which will train you, get you through the exam, and offer you work on their routes (assuming you pass your training). You don't need to pay the cost of training, but you will be committed to working for a minimum length of time with the company once you have passed the exam and their other training courses. The other way to train is to go to a specialist driving school and pay the fees yourself. These are about £1,000; the course takes about ten to fifteen days, depending on how well you get on. Once qualified, you gain experience on shorter, local trips before progressing to long-distance or Continental driving.

WHAT'S IT LIKE?

Peter left an office job to become a coach driver: 'I tried to get a job as a rep in a holiday resort, but they said to go away and work in another travel job first, so I got a job with a bus company. They got me through my PCV, then I spent two years working the same routes. I had to do two years or they took back the cost of my training. I liked the driving but the passengers drove me mad. I realised it wasn't what I wanted to do. I knew then why they didn't take me as a rep: I haven't got enough patience with people. I moved to a coach company on day trips, then on to longer routes with a courier on board, and that was much better. There's someone else "on your side" then, and they deal with the problems, instead of the driver. I enjoyed that, but stopped in the end as

I did the same routes too many times. But the PCV is still useful and I use that now in my work at an FE college.'

Other drivers speak of the freedom of being on the road, the atmosphere when there's a courier and a good group on board, and the pleasure of seeing new sights. Drawbacks include the stress of driving new roads without anyone to navigate, noisy or disruptive passengers, sitting for long periods, and hanging around while passengers spend time at a sight or attraction.

SKILLS YOU'LL NEED

You must be at least 18 to gain your PCV, and then you can only drive local bus services until you are 21. 'Driving skills are important,' says Chris Chatfield, 'but they're not enough. You need to keep a cool head, and not get wound up with the roads or the passengers.' You're also working on your own, so you need to be self-reliant, punctual and polite. 'You need a basic geographical knowledge,' continues Chris. 'You can't sit with a map on your knee and not know where to go.'

If you start with a bus company you need to be able to handle money, but otherwise there's no call for numeracy or academic skills, so you won't need any qualifications apart from your clean driving licence, probably gained a few years beforehand to give you enough basic driving experience. You also need to have worked with the public at some stage, to show that you are proficient in a customer service role.

You need to be able to cope with long hours sitting and long spells away from home, with loading and unloading luggage, and with hanging around for hours while everyone else goes off and enjoys themselves. You will almost certainly wear a uniform.

PRACTICAL INSIDER INFORMATION ON HOW TO GET THE JOB

Most people pay for their own training. TRANSfED (see below) can supply a list of approved driving schools. Otherwise, contact your local bus companies for details of their driver training schemes. It'll help if you have plenty of driving experience and have driven a minibus or van.

Experienced drivers are generally more in demand, but as Chris says: 'I do sometimes look for newly qualified people as I can train them up. Sometimes more experienced people are stuck in their ways.'

USEFUL ADDRESSES

● TRANSfED has details of training courses. Try their website or contact them at:
43 High Street, Rickmansworth,
WD3 1ET.
Tel: 01923 896607.
www.transfed.org.uk

CONTRACTOR

Contractors, or contracts managers, are part of the core of tour operating. They are the people who go out to resort and book capacity in the best hotels at the best possible prices. They sign deals on the spot so that they can be incorporated into the planning, the hotels can be written into the brochures, and the holidays sold.

It's not a job for a newcomer: you'll have to be experienced, and good at what you do. That experience is certain to include time working overseas, as it's hard to truly understand how the resort business works otherwise. You also rely on the support of the resort teams, and they won't have much respect for you unless you know from the inside how it works.

Contractors quite often go away for three or four weeks at a time. Each contracts manager has an area – perhaps the Balearics or Tunisia or North Africa, depending on the number of resorts and the size of the operation. You'll blitz an area and its resorts, looking at the properties on offer: hotels, apartment complexes and so on. You might visit six properties a day, maybe more, or spend a full day looking over a new property. If a property is already represented by the company, then it might be just a quick look around – a chat about price, sign on the line, arrange dinner for later, perhaps, and on to the next. If the property has become run-down you might have to say no to it and look elsewhere. You'll view new properties, looking for all the obvious things such as quality of food and accommodation. You'll also check that they comply with health and safety requirements, as tour operators are now responsible in law for the safety of the properties they send their customers to.

You also need to get the 'feel' of the place: does it fit the programme that your company is building? Will it suit the target clients? Will it be too upmarket/downmarket? 'You need a vision, as a contracts manager, of how and what and who you're buying for – it's like shopping: you shop around and you pick one you like and you buy it.' So says Doranne Reid, a contractor-in-training planning to make the jump to contracts manager once she has enough experience. She works for the Panorama Holiday Group as their Contracts Co-ordinator. After viewing the property, she says, 'contractors haggle. British tour operators are known as being particularly hard negotiators, though less so these days as other nationalities' tour operators push harder. We would always get the best rates. A lot of hoteliers are conscious of who they want in their hotels. They understand that it's not in their best interests to have a hundred per cent of one nationality occupying their hotels, because if something goes wrong in that country, anything could happen.

'The accommodation contract is signed there and then. If you're signing a five-year deal it could be an enormous amount of money. There's a lot of responsibility. There are two types of contract: Guaranteed and On Release. With a guaranteed contract we would pay whether we sell the beds or not. More often we would have contracts on release, where we give the rooms back if we don't sell them in a certain time.'

After a long day's negotiating there's the obligatory wining and dining: relationships with hoteliers are very important and it's up to you to maintain these. Hospitality is much more common in countries such as India, where tourism is a growing part of the economy and where relationships with tour operators are very important, but less frequent in areas such as the Balearics. There the product is already 'sold' to the British public and hoteliers can choose which tour operators they use to a large extent. It's becoming increasingly difficult to find any beds at all, let alone good ones, in some of these areas. Some tour operators are now buying hotel complexes so that they are assured of the beds.

CO-ORDINATING THE CONTACTS

'We have a team of contracts managers and I am the back-up in the UK,' explains Doranne. 'A contract with a hotel could be for anything from six months to five years. It would say how many rooms are allocated per week, the cost of the rooms and details of any special offers to the tour operator, which we would then give to the client via the brochure.

'The contracts managers bring back the contracts and I then distribute them around the building to Brochure Production, to Commercial and the accounts department, so that they can be logged on to the systems. They also bring back transparencies of the hotels, hotel information, and anything new for the brochure. They give them to me and I make sure that they go to the relevant departments.

'Suppliers may phone up about an accounts problem, or might say: "I hate that picture you've got in the brochure", or: "I've got a special offer for you". You need to be very good on the phone and it helps if you can say hello and goodbye in different languages, though most of them speak English. There's a lot of administration and paperwork. As I'm training to be a contracts manager I get to go out in the field and look at the resorts. It's important to know when somebody mentions the name of the hotel that that's in that resort in that country. It's a very interesting job.'

NEW MARKETS

Contractors therefore set the whole tone of the product via the properties they choose; their negotiating skills help determine brochure prices and profitability. A mistake can be very costly for the company, not just in terms of paying over the odds for the beds but if it becomes the subject of complaints or accidents.

Contracts managers also research new areas for the company to move into. 'There are always new countries and properties being contracted,' says Doranne. 'We research into other operators and where they go, to find out what the market is doing. We've got a big brochure file of all our competitors' brochures. We look as a company to where our market is: we are very successful in Tunisia, now we've gone to Morocco. Where do we go from there?'

It looks as though contracting will become more difficult in the future. Says Doranne: 'It's very competitive in areas such as the Canaries. Everyone wants the best beds; everyone is fighting for the same thing. Also, with the new way people are contracting five-year periods, a hotel is completely off your list for another five years, signed up to another company. There are more and more of these long deals taking place. Anything that is left will be what nobody wants.'

Contracting is a fabulous job from the point of view of travel, though sometimes contractors feel they are never at home. But a manager has a lot of freedom. As Doranne puts it: 'They're a bit like special agents: they're out on a mission, and however they do it is up to them, as long as they come up with the goods at the end.'

SKILLS YOU'LL NEED

Doranne reckons that 'you need to be outgoing and friendly, but there are many different personalities within contracting so it's difficult to pigeonhole: some are quiet and some completely outrageous, but they have one common denominator – a love of travel, of going away, of discovery.'

You need to be very experienced and of high calibre: at Panorama, the managing director does the contracting for one destination. You don't need a legal background but need to understand health, fire and safety, and on the accounts side you've got to be good at figures. Generally you need some overseas experience. You don't get young contractors – they tend to be from age 30 up. You need to be ambitious, to have drive.

'I speak French and a bit of Tunisian Arabic, but I don't need it,' says Doranne. 'You start off in their language and finish in English. Negotiations should be in English anyway because I need to feel a hundred per cent secure and I would be better in English than in any other language. If a hotelier wants the business then he or she should be represented by someone who speaks English. It gives you control over the situation.'

PRACTICAL INSIDER INFORMATION ON HOW TO GET THE JOB

If you want something badly enough it's a matter of proving yourself. Doranne was a top hairdresser and taught at the London College of Fashion before going overseas as a rep for four years. Then she came back and spent a year in Panorama's commercial department, learning how tour operation really worked. 'I saw my time in commercial as doing time, but it paid off. It's hard to change career later on in life: you have to be prepared to compromise.'

CRUISE STAFF

TRAVEL RATING: 8/10 – you'll see the world ... but check that your contract allows you to leave the ship or it'll be through salt-encrusted portholes.

MONEY: Varies enormously. One operator starts staff on £20,000 a year. Others pay a bare minimum and expect staff to make their wages up with tips.

HOURS: Possibly sixteen-hour days, maybe very little time off to enjoy the places you visit. Maybe on a rota system, where you have equal time on leave and on board; maybe not.

HEALTH RISK: 5/10. Cruise ships are clean and luxurious places: companies cannot afford to be sued by their passengers. But the crew's quarters and food, though clean, are in a different category, and you may find it difficult to remain sane for long periods below deck in cramped conditions and close proximity to humankind.

PRESSURE RATING: 8/10. Hard work, cramped quarters and constant contact with rich bastards make it a tough job.

GLAMOUR RATING: 3–6/10. The places the ship visits are fantastic. The work can be fulfilling, though often isn't. The lifestyle suits some people very well, others not at all.

A cruise ship is a strange place. It's similar, in some ways, to a crowded holiday resort, but where no one can escape and where you work long hours serving people you wouldn't normally want to be anywhere near. There are loads of different ranks and categories of work, and your enjoyment on board depends on what you do and the status you have. The experience is unbeatable, though some people who've worked cruises feel that the cost is too high.

Cruise work can be divided into two areas: the technical side, which means sailing the ship and associated activities, and the hotel side. This section deals mostly with hotel-type work. See the piece at the end of this section for an overview of the technical side, and where to find out more.

The cruise market is an increasingly important one: cruise lines are having more and larger ships built, and more of us want to spend our holidays on them. Even though you probably won't get work on a cruise ship without experience in the travel or hospitality industries, the sector is growing so fast that you'll probably consider it after working for some time in other areas.

Most 'hotel' cruise work is similar to work in other areas of the travel business, and includes the following categories:

● Waiters: known as stewards, and traditionally a male job, though women also do this work now. You need at least one additional language, plus experience in a top-class hotel and the training that goes with that.

● Cabin attendants: also known as stewards and also mainly men. Again you'll need good hotel experience to get work here, plus another language. You'll clean and service the passenger cabins and provide room service.

● Pursers: these are effectively ships' managers. You'll start as an assistant purser after doing similar work on land, probably in hotel reception or in general management, perhaps in another customer service role. Duties include buying, personnel, reception, information work, sorting out problems and complaints, and managing all the facilities on board. You'll need another language, A levels or a GNVQ, and probably a degree.

● Chefs/catering assistants: cruise passengers' main pastime is eating, and the kitchens are rarely closed. You'll need the same experience and qualifications as you would to join a top hotel, though assistants won't need the qualifications.

● Croupiers: every cruise ship has at least one casino and needs croupiers. You'll have started as a trainee with an onshore casino and gained your Gaming Board licence, then probably clocked up additional experience.

● Entertainers: see the separate section for information about this.

● Health club staff: there's a big demand for health and beauty treatments and sports tuition, as well as games and tournaments. These are usually run by other companies as concessions, meaning that the cruise line itself doesn't employ you. You'll need the relevant qualifications and experience for the work you do.

● Sales staff: there are many shops on board, again often run as concessions (see above).

WHAT'S IT LIKE ON BOARD?

'Passengers don't know about the hard work that goes on behind the scenes,' says Mike Wood, marketing director of Fjordline. His company operates cruise ferries between the UK and Norway, plus other routes. These trips are run both as ferries and as cruises. On cruises, passengers have several days admiring the fjords from the ship then spend a limited time ashore before returning. The ships have 170 crew members in total and carry 1,200 passengers. 'All crew positions are doubled off,' says Mike. 'This means that two crew members have the same job and arrange between themselves when they will each work.' Some pairs choose to work two weeks on then two weeks off. Others alternate in monthly cycles. This is more common on the longer routes. 'The crew live on the ship all the time they are on duty,' says Mike, 'although on the winter schedule they may have some time off the boat. They have their own crew **mess**, bar, laundry, and so on.' The officers all have single cabins though some of the other crew share. 'But single accommodation is becoming more common these days,' says Mike. 'New ships are being built with single cabins for crew.'

The hours are long, but then you might have the whole of the next month off. 'People either take to it very quickly, or not at all,' says Mike. 'Some people have come off ships in a matter of weeks. It's glamorous from the outside but to insiders, no, it's not. It's about being a team. A lot of people on board don't have strong family connections, and the crew are their family. How you get on with this depends on your disposition.'

Cruise lines vary in their policies on crew mixing with the passengers. Many do not encourage or allow this, while others let you make your own choice. 'Some crew like mixing with the passengers,' says Mike, 'and others keep themselves to themselves and don't socialise with the passengers.'

Dave Manning, a musician who worked on an American cruise ship (see Entertainer section), says: 'The passengers were thick as shit. There were so many horrible, uncultured people who would rather stay in an air-conditioned restaurant below decks than go out on to a beautiful island that had no shops. They weren't nasty people; they were all very polite, but we were patronised for being English: "Is England near London?", "Do you know Prince Charles?" It brings out your Englishness. They thought we were very quaint. We were always polite, but it was a strain.'

Whatever it's like mingling, there's a great social life for crew below decks, and most people love the atmosphere.

A CAUTIONARY TALE

There are some fantastic cruise ships sailing the world. Most operate out of Miami in the USA, though some sail from European ports. They are small islands of luxury, and many are run to the highest standards throughout. However, as with any commercial organisation, they are there to make a profit. Some American ships are having increasing problems getting good crew, because, in the words of one insider: 'It's not the job that it used to be. Tips used to be very, very strong but they are less so, now. The huge cruise ships have traditionally relied on cheap labour from the Caribbean.' As this labour is less available, some cruise lines are turning to agencies recruiting from around the world.

A former cruise worker explains how one US cruise line works: 'I worked as a cocktail waiter. I found work easily because I have good experience and good references, so I negotiated a good contract. After I'd been there a while I discovered that some of the international staff, which meant mainly the stewards, were recruited on a no-wage contract. They went through agencies in their home countries, which might be Lithuania or Japan or anywhere: France, even the UK. They'd been promised "pay plus tips" of up to $1,000 a week, but they didn't tell them there was no basic wage at all, just their keep.

'They worked eighteen-hour days, got four hours' sleep and one morning off a week. They kept going on vitamin tablets. Because they're dependent on tips, they're lovely and polite. That's how the cruise line keeps its "standards". If a passenger complains or they get less than top in their customer feedback forms, they risk the sack. Then they'll be put off at the next port and have to find their own passage home. The whole system is geared up for people to knuckle under and behave themselves. As a French guy I met said: "I have no choice, I'm stuck here". Tipping's built into the US culture. Passengers are given guidelines on tipping: it's about three dollars per passenger per day, but they don't have to give you anything.'

Don't be put off! Many companies do not work this way. Just ensure you read your contract very carefully and. if possible, get advice from people experienced in how the cruise industry works.

TRAVEL

'It's a great way to see the world,' says Mike Wood. 'You can get a lot of time onshore at either end, and can really make the most of it. Though a lot of ports tend to look the same after a while. Also, someone has to work while the ship's in port.' Again, check your contract to find out whether you will have access to the places you visit.

SKILLS YOU'LL NEED

For all these roles, at least one additional language is usually necessary. Your languages will affect where you work: some ships have mainly English-speaking passengers plus a good proportion of Spanish-speaking, for instance. Others might be mostly French or Italian. For safety reasons, you will need to speak the language spoken by the officers who run the ship. Fjordline, for instance, being Norwegian-owned and -run, insists that all crew have a Scandinavian language. 'We have certain language tests when we're recruiting,' says Mike Wood. 'People don't need to be fluent but they do need to clearly understand the language in an emergency situation. British people who work for us tend to have Norwegian parents or have worked over there and gained the language.'

See the job headings above for levels of experience. In addition, Mike Wood says: 'Qualifications required depend on the levels of experience and the job. In housekeeping, qualifications requirements are not so high; instead we are looking for qualities such as innovation. You've got to have the discipline to work closely with people, who become like your family. So you've got to get on with people. You've got to be flexible, because if the ship is delayed you have to accept that you will work extra hours. It's the nature of the business. You've got to be customer-focused.' There may be a minimum age, perhaps 21, though it's unlikely you would have sufficient experience and maturity before this to get a job on board anyway.

Educational requirements vary as you may well be working for a foreign-owned and -run company, with different requirements to the UK norms. Some cruise lines require a minimum educational level of four GCSEs at grade C or above, including maths and English. Others do not stipulate a minimum. At Fjordline, new entrants into management roles require an MBA (Master of Business Administration degree, a postgraduate business qualification). This is not the norm for UK companies but, as Mike Wood says: 'This is more a Norwegian requirement. It's not standard in the UK yet but we are going that way.'

PRACTICAL INSIDER INFORMATION ON HOW TO GET THE JOB

For all this work, the highest standards of qualification, or at least of experience, are required, and there is fierce competition for the work. You won't go straight from education into cruise ships, and the time you spend in hotels or other work first will give you a chance to find out about the career opportunities on board.

Very few vacancies are advertised: most are filled through the cruise employment agencies and direct applications on spec to the cruise lines. Most positions are offered on six- or twelve-month contracts, though the length of contract varies depending on the type and length of cruise.

NB: Most cruise ships operate from the USA, and you may have to apply to a company based there. You'll need a listing of organisations: ask at your reference library for a book specifically about working on cruise ships.

A BIT ABOUT THE TECHNICAL SIDE OF CRUISE SHIPS

People who run the technical side of cruise ships come through the shipping industry. Jobs range from captain to deck-hands and greasers (people who work in the engine rooms). You'll be trained before you go on board because of safety requirements, though there'll be on-going training once you're there.

Perhaps you'll start as a naval cadet in the merchant navy after a spell at a specialist college, or take a cadet course with a major shipping line. You might already be an electrician and want to retrain in maritime electrical engineering, or you might go to maritime college and train as a maritime engineer.

Information about training and careers is available through the major shipping lines and the maritime colleges, which are based in the principal ports. Ask your careers adviser for addresses, or go on-line and start from there. Try the website of the Chamber of Shipping and its links to colleges: www.british-shipping.org/training/index.htm

GLOSSARY
● **Mess**
Something your shared cabin must never be ... and a place on board ship where crews eat and socialise.

ENTERTAINER

The travel business uses entertainers to keep its customers happy and relaxed: it's a vital part of holidays such as packages to large resorts, and cruises. You'll also find entertainers in holiday camps, hotels, bars, nightclubs and ferries, and almost anywhere else, around the world.

If you want to be on-stage, you know it. It's not a career option you first consider along with management training schemes at age eighteen. Andrew Farr explains why people want to do it: 'It's winning people over all the time, that terrible actor thing. You're looking for something out of people.' For the many thousands of people who want to make it in showbiz, the travel industry can be the start of their brilliant career. It offers one of the chances to gain an 'apprenticeship' tapping the boards (or whatever your speciality), sometimes leading to an **Equity card**.

Others simply enjoy entertaining, are of a professional standard and want to give it a go and see where it leads. There's room for people like this in travel, too.

Andrew Farr first thought about repping, and the entertainment possibilities that it held, when, after graduating, he worked the Christmas season at Boots the Chemist. 'I was working on a counter in the toy department and to liven things up did a cash-and-wrap bingo; my manager suggested I applied for a rep job. It was a general representative but in those days we didn't really have entertainers. Then the whole rep thing was to be more entertaining; now the feel of people going on holiday has changed. Then we were expected to give people good information but at the same time give people fun; it tends to be more serious now.' He points out the similarities between repping and entertaining: 'It's being the centre of attention: you become a very big fish in a small pond, which is what you are on-stage with people looking at you all the time. All the time as a rep, I was always wanting to be liked by everybody.'

Perhaps because of the changing nature of a rep's work and the more sober approach that customers want, larger tour operators now recruit people specifically to be Entertainer Reps and focus on the fun side, while the mainstream reps take a back-seat role. 'They work in the larger hotels,' says Andrew, 'particularly the hotels where the atmosphere is a bit like Butlins. At first they used to take keen amateurs but now they actually search for people with qualifications in dance and music. They are in charge of up to four or five hundred guests and organise the daytime activities, then go on-stage two or three times a week. They do a very professional cabaret. It's a good way of starting out, and will be a growing sector.'

There are still opportunities to combine the main repping role with being an entertainer if you work in a smaller resort or with a smaller tour operator: 'I did a stint in Kerkenna for three months,' remembers Andrew. 'I was the only rep so I did everything, including entertainments, which was great for me, because after two years I came back to the UK to work in theatre.'

Andrew does have words of caution about the entertainment work, though: 'I don't know many reps who've enjoyed doing reps' cabarets. Our cabarets in Tunisia are held in a good venue, and are professionally put on, but even though I've done a lot of work

in the theatre I wasn't comfortable doing it. So it's good that larger companies are moving away from reps' cabarets as well as from bingo every night.'

Another halfway job is to work as a youth market rep. This role combines non-stop entertainment with responsibility for looking after groups of 15–25-year-olds.

SAILING

Another entertainer to find work through the travel business is Dave Manning. Dave is a professional musician who works as a freelance drummer, plays in a number of bands, does general recording work for songwriters, and teaches. 'One day I'll be playing hip hop in a nightclub,' he says, 'and the next day I'll be playing jazz in a hotel wearing a bow tie.' When the opportunity arose to work on a ship in the Caribbean, he couldn't refuse. It was an eight-day cruise, organised by his band leader through an **agent**. The cruise line wanted a specialist jazz band to play in one of the ship's many bars.

Dave and the rest of the band flew out to Puerto Rico, where they boarded ship. They were allocated passenger cabins and mingled freely with the paying guests: 'It was a massive, American-owned ship with eleven passenger decks,' remembers Dave. 'Each deck had its own restaurants, clubs and bars.' The entertainers ranged from jugglers and cabaret artistes through to celebrities. Among the fifteen bands were a number of 'cabaret bands'. They're on long-term contracts, and they back other musicians and acts. They have to be extremely versatile and excellent sight-readers. 'These people work very hard, with six sets totalling up to five hours a day playing time, with hardly any days off,' says Dave. 'They might do cheesy jazz during dinner then flat-out rock 'n' roll later. It's the hardest job.' There were also solo pianists in the bars and foyers, and a range of other entertainers.

'My band was hired to play a certain type of music in a certain bar. It was unbelievably easy. We only worked forty-five minutes a day starting at about midnight. We were hired to play until the guests went to bed, but they all went by one a.m. So we stopped playing.' There's no real rule: Dave's contract specified more work, but in the end this was all that was required.

'We had full passenger status,' remembers Dave, 'which is quite unusual. There are so many different ways of getting on cruises. If your band's got a reputation and you get approached, you can barter for better wages, cabin status, food, and so on. The other extreme is to work as part of a band on a ship with crew status, maybe sharing four to a tiny cabin for months on end. Every case is different. You can have a really hard time.' Dave's passenger status allowed him and the band to leave the ship at its ports of call, to swim and lie around in the sun.

'The secret is to be a true entertainer,' says Dave. 'You please the public, you look who's dancing and who isn't, and make sure that everyone's happy. You're not there to perform your art; you're there to entertain. You do get a lot of musicians who think it's demeaning, but it's not art: it's entertainment. If you want to do your own art, do it somewhere else. There are two types of musician, those who go after stardom, and working musicians. I don't care about the glamour, that's not the purpose. Most working musicians don't even think about that.

'I personally find this sort of work very satisfying; I like the variety. But I couldn't do anything every day. It would do my head in.'

Dave also worked a 'cruise to nowhere' one New Year. He drove to Hull, boarded the boat with the guests, 'went to sea, sailed around a bit, played and did the New Year celebrations, went back to port and got off the next day. I was part of a function band, which means we try to cater to as many people as possible, from thirties tunes through to chart hits.'

FULL-TIME ENTERTAINERS

Cruise ships have their own entertainers, known as entertainment staff. They organise and run the entertainments on board ship, and although they book in professional entertainers, on smaller ships and as needed they get up on-stage themselves. The people in charge of the entertainment staff are called Entertainments Managers. They have overall responsibility for booking in entertainers, negotiating their pay and conditions, ensuring their papers are in order (they might need passports and visas, for instance), allocating accommodation, and supervising everything. It all has to run like clockwork, and the logistics can be very complex on a large ship. 'They've got a lot of power,' says Dave. 'They're in complete control. They might be dealing with fifteen bands plus the nannies in the crèche, the magicians, and all the other entertainers. Artistes are strong-willed and flappy people; they need to be directed but you also need a lot of tact. You need very good leadership qualities to do that job.'

OTHER OPPORTUNITIES

There's also entertainment work within the travel business in the UK, as Tracy Turki found out when she left a dull job to spend a season in a UK holiday camp: 'The work was very clerical, and suddenly overnight we didn't have much to do, so I decided to get out while I could. From there I became a Pontins Bluecoat. Bluecoats do the entertaining. A lot of people who've done Bluecoat work, or other work in the UK holiday industry, then get the bug to try something abroad. I worked just one season, that was all I could physically do; I was absolutely exhausted after that.' Tracy had already applied for a job as a rep overseas. 'Even though it was exhausting it was still good. Civil servant to Bluecoat was something totally different and, once I'd got into entertaining people, like a lot of people I went on from that to working overseas. Others carried on in British holiday camps.'

Other entertainers work the world's hotels. Particularly busy areas include parts of the Middle East, especially Bahrain and Dubai. Entertainers are typically paid £500 a week plus a daily £50 food allowance, and are normally on three-month contracts. Says Dave Manning: 'You're very well looked after. There are loads of hotels mainly for Westerners, and a mass of entertainments.'

SKILLS YOU'LL NEED

You must be able to entertain like a pro, not like you're dressed up in front of your bedroom mirror. You'll probably need UK experience before you hit the rest of the world. If you are unsure about your employability with a particular type of act, contact an entertainer's employment agency and ask them.

Beyond this, you need the qualities of anyone working with the public, especially if your role is not solely stage work. 'You need all the normal professional attributes,' says Dave Manning. 'You need to be punctual, polite, presentable, able to cope with people who are stressed. As a musician you need versatility, especially in a cabaret band.' You may need another language, depending where you are working, and you'll need to be organised with good administrative skills for some roles.

PRACTICAL INSIDER INFORMATION ON HOW TO GET THE JOB

'Be very well prepared,' says Andrew. 'Even though recruiters stress that people will need to prepare something to perform, it's amazing how many people don't. We want to say to them: "Why haven't you got anything prepared?" We're looking for very slick acts now. Everyone wants to do it; it's perceived as glamorous (despite what they pay).'

Write to the larger tour operators and the cruise companies for vacancy details. Contact agencies and talk to the staff there. Any one agency will probably place people in a variety of work, possibly including cruises as well as hotels and clubs. Agencies vary from a local bloke who fills a couple of clubs to massive agencies supplying people to play Wembley. Vacancies are rarely advertised and you may have to phone or write on spec to find out what's available. 'It's quite hard to find work with agencies,' says Dave. 'You usually have more than one, especially initially.

'You have to build a relationship with an agent, then they know you have all the right qualities. If you were to get sacked, then you wouldn't get paid and the agency would lose its reputation and wouldn't get their commission. They need to believe in you.'

To get work with an agent you need to supply a CD or video of your work, photographs and a CV. Established agencies might try you out on smaller contracts to start with, but if they're desperate because they've been let down, you might get thrown in at the deep end. Then, if you do well, they'll give you more work. There's lots of feedback between the venues and the agents.

'A lot of musicians will be on stand-by with agencies,' explains Dave, 'and are willing to go on a cruise at a day's notice, perhaps for a six- or eight-month contract. This may be necessary because sometimes the

entertainers on board ship go mad. They fall out with people, get drunk, end up hitting people and get sacked. I was with my best mates, and I couldn't have handled more than four weeks of it.' They, and their replacements, 'tend to earn less and have less bargaining power than if you're approached by an agent'. But this is a good way of starting out. If you earn a good reputation for your musicianship and professionalism, employers will start to ask for you. 'But some entertainers have been wiped clean by doing it for too long,' says Dave. 'They stand on-stage and they're dross.'

GLOSSARY
● **Agent**
Music and entertainment agents find work for people in the entertainment business through their contacts with the venues. They take a percentage of what the entertainer earns – the standard percentage is 15 per cent.
● **Equity card**
Equity is the performers' union. You must be a member before you can take up acting work, but you need the experience before you can get membership ... Read up about this complex issue in a specialist publication.

ENTREPRENEUR

Entrepreneurs are people who start up businesses. There are thousands in the travel industry, most operating on a small scale. But the major companies and groups in the travel business today all contain businesses that started small and have grown to their current size, usually over many years.

Michael Brunt started his travel agency working from home seven years ago. It has now developed into a small business specialising in travel to Portugal. He also puts holidays together for customers, marrying accommodation and travel as a package. He describes how his business started: 'I didn't have the faintest idea about travel when I started this. Some airline company staff came to me who'd left their company and wanted to start a travel club doing basically what I'm doing now, selling cheap flights to members. About a year later they got fed up because they weren't making much money. They chucked it in and said: "If you want it, take it over."

'They had the accounts dealing with the people who sell flights. I took over their account numbers and advertised. I didn't make much money initially because a travel club was too much to run and maintain. I thought: I can't see any point advertising to members of a club. All the money was being spent on flashy paper and so on, telling members that we were a specialist. Why not just advertise in Yellow Pages? That turned it around and away I went.

'It took four years until it was a

reasonable business. Then I bought another business. I wasn't looking to but I would probably have folded if I hadn't. A contact had his own business dealing with accommodation in Portugal and wanted to sell. He felt it would fit with my business. He then wrote to all the hotels and blocks of apartments and gave them my name, and I went from there. I was just doing flights before that. I'm now putting flights together with accommodation.'

For Michael, working from home is an advantage and allows him to give customers extra service over his competitors. When he first advertised he stated that his was a twenty-four-hour service, and he's prepared to answer the phone at any time of the day or night: 'You're here all the time if there are problems. You could do it from an office but there are so many different outlets, you need to get one over on them. I also advertise last-minute flights in the Yellow Pages for anyone who wants to go tomorrow. Travel agents all do this but most of them don't advertise it. And lots of travel agents won't ring customers back.'

Excellent service has been what's given Michael's agency the edge over the high-street competition. But it hasn't been easy. 'I put an awful lot into this because once you've built up an initial bunch of customers they'll keep coming back. But I've never been to Portugal. Being a one-man band, how do I get up and go with tickets coming through the door all the time?'

He manages by doing everything himself, acquiring and teaching himself to use new software packages to enable him to make the most of the new technology. 'I do all my accounting on my PC; I fax the hotels in the evenings, and using e-mail cuts the costs down.' He's also looking ahead: 'I expanded the Portugal business: I bought into it by going to the Travel Show in London and going to the Portugal stand, where there were different sets of accommodation looking for people like me to represent them over here.' It's clearly hard work, but as Michael says: 'When I get customers ringing to say what a beautiful hotel it was, I think: I'm doing something right here.'

TOUR OPERATING

Although travel insiders say that it is much easier to set up in the travel business with some experience of the industry, it's not uncommon to find people like Michael who have done it the hard way, and learned as they went along. Two people who got plenty of travel experience first are Justin Fleming and Nick Munday. Their business also flourished, and the Panorama Holiday Group is now a major tour operator. Justin started off in the travel business working as an assistant to the managing director of a small tour company, Panorama. 'After about eighteen months I became general manager of the tour operation and I was responsible to the director for most of the tour operation in terms of producing the brochure, buying aircraft seats, and making sure it ran. Travel wasn't so complicated then. Generally speaking, demand exceeded supply, so whatever you put together in a brochure you probably didn't have to do much to sell; you sent the brochure out and bookings came in and that was it, really. There wasn't a great shortage of beds or aircraft seats so you could get all the ingredients, and there weren't any computers or anything like that so you didn't need any particular IT skills. I seem to remember we didn't even have a photocopier when I first started.'

That company did well, but it wasn't going to keep Justin happy for ever: 'I stayed for ten years and became a director of the company, and then I thought at age thirty-five where was I going to go with my career and my business life? The company was family-owned and was in fact contracting, so I decided to start my own business. I wanted to create a specialist tour operator to Tunisia. Specialisation was the way to go in a big marketplace, and I felt that I was able to run my own business, as I'd done it in the past. I bought the major part of a friend's small company, Ski Young World, started Tunisia Experience, opened a travel shop and carried on with the ski programme.'

He started off with one assistant. Then his wife joined him and, eighteen months later, so did Nick. Together they bought Panorama and renamed it Panorama Holidays, then developed more programmes. They built the business over the next twelve years, during which time Justin's role grew from being managing director with one member of staff to being MD of a company that was carrying 160,000 passengers and employing 200 staff in the UK and overseas.

Justin's business partner, Nick, always had a burning ambition to run his own company. 'We were so single-minded that nothing was going to stop us. It was terrible for our health and family life, for twelve years of running our own business. We could have failed numerous times if we'd been prepared to accept failure, which we weren't. Though we were lucky, as well as working extremely hard. It was worth it – we loved every minute of it; it was great fun, a great experience.'

Eighteen months ago, Nick and Justin sold their business to Airtours, a major holiday group, though they still run the company. Nick says of this: 'The way it ended was great. It was the best part of the whole thing. If we'd sold, made a lot of money, left our workmates in the lurch and seen the company being destroyed it would have been terrible. Ninety-nine per cent of the time that's what happens. The new owners usually believe that they have to do something to change the business to make it even better, and usually the entrepreneur can't work with the new owner because the entrepreneur is used to running his own show, so he leaves within three months. Then follow all kinds of barmy decisions and the company goes to the wall or is merged in. Eighteen months down the line here, the business is three times bigger and people are thriving. There haven't been any casualties at all; that's pretty unique really. I could walk out tomorrow and feel comfortable with that fact that we built the business, sold it at the peak and eighteen months later it's a better business. Airtours, me and the staff are all happy. That is a perfect outcome.'

SKILLS YOU'LL NEED

There's a myriad of skills you need in order to be a successful entrepreneur. If you're thinking of taking the plunge, start to research, research, research. Buy a specialist book and go to your local enterprise people – look in the phone book, or find them via your JobCentre – and talk to them. It'll become clear what sort of person you need to be and the skills you should have. As far as specific 'technical' skills go, you'll need:

● Up-to-date software skills.
● Languages, if you are dealing with people abroad who don't speak English.
● Numeracy: like it or not, you'll end up needing to understand numbers and accounts.
● Literacy and presentation skills: vital if you're going to sell yourself and your product.
● Contacts: always.

PRACTICAL INSIDER INFORMATION ON HOW TO GET THE JOB

Michael:

● 'I wouldn't advise people to do travel on their own; there's too much competition. You wouldn't make any money out of it. If you do, try and specialise: don't try and do accommodation all over the world or you will come a cropper, because you're trying to deal with so many people and currencies.'

● 'Trying to do it yourself is definitely not simple and you need another input of cash until you get going.'

● 'When people go on travel courses they get PC training – everything is driven by the PC. It's just mundane sort of stuff: all the packages arrive on CD-ROMs and you can set up your own business quite easily.'

● 'If you've got contacts with the accommodation you can sell it and people can get their own flights easily enough, but with getting accommodation, the knowledge of where it is and the facilities offered are more important.'

Nick:

● 'I don't think in business there's any substitute for honesty, integrity and hard work. There's no easy win, no matter what business you're in.'

● 'The only way to succeed in business is by being better than your competitors. They can mimic you extremely quickly. Any advantage which you create in any way at all, in efficiency or your product or whatever, is eroded in a matter of weeks. So in business you've got to be entrepreneurial and have vision and flair, but you've got to run it properly.'

● 'Becoming an entrepreneur like Justin or myself is still possible now. People who want to get into this, they either need to be massive or to have a niche. If you try to imitate the big people you can't win: you need to have phenomenal money and you're playing in the big league where really you're just playing with numbers, where it's not real money, it's just accounting entries.'

● 'With e-commerce and the way that tourism is developing with low-cost carriers, there's more opportunity to think of new products now than when we set up. Then, we had to sell

through travel agents and we had to
buy from competitors' airlines
because that was the only way of
getting any seats.'

● 'People setting up in business
employ people who they get on well
with because it's nice to work with
people who think you're great. It's
nothing to do with whether they
know anything.'

● 'When you've worked twenty years
in this business you think you've got
all the answers, but you haven't,
because tomorrow's problem will be
different to today's.'

E-TRAVEL

TRAVEL RATING: 2/10. From the bus to the office, the office to the bus ...

MONEY: Millions have been made by a motivated and lucky few with **dot.com** flotations. Otherwise, 'anyone who's going to work in travel, including **IT** in travel, has got to work quite long hours probably for lower-than-average pay.'

HOURS: This can be deadline work. Even when it's not, you will have that look skiers have around their eyes, but on you it will be all over.

HEALTH RISK: 6/10. You'll need specs after a few years of this; you'll eat too much junk, drink too much and never get any exercise. And meeting a travel agent at a party could have serious health repercussions.

PRESSURE RATING: 5–10/10. High around deadline time. High around flotation time. High around year-end and targets time … But there are mainstream IT roles as there are in any industry, with no more pressure than average.

GLAMOUR RATING: 5–10/10. Anything with a dot.com suffix is cool. Add travel, and you've got the glammest of the glam. And you don't have to wear an anorak these days.

New technology and the travel business are solid partners. IT underpins every part of the industry. It's transforming 'retail' into something new: it's now possible to buy almost any travel product 'direct', thus cutting out the middleman (the travel agent). New and better systems underpin the work of tour operators and suppliers such as airlines. Technology people – e-travel people – make this possible.

Every tour operator of any size has a website run by a communications technology person or department, and is looking at how it can use this technology to cut costs. A major cost-cutting exercise is getting customers to book direct so it does not need to pay commission to travel agents. 'The thing that most enthuses travel companies about IT at the moment,' says Paul Richer, senior partner of travel technology consultancy Genesys, 'is its distribution opportunities – that is, selling the product – thanks to the Web, digital TV and Internet-enabled mobile phones. It gets board directors excited; it's where the corporate focus is.'

Travel's internal workings are also highly systemised. To make a business work, computers have to be effective, and programs become more and more complex. Now agents, tour operators and airlines offer pre-booked seats on aircraft, different types of seats at different prices, and an array of other extras that wouldn't be possible without the booking technology. Organisations and their networks grow and need more complex IT input and back-up. Airports get busier and air traffic control systems become larger.

'In-house IT is growing in importance,' says one insider. 'You need to be able to work as fast as people expect of you. Maintaining all your servers, your databases, reservations systems, internal communication systems: that's a growing part of the business.'

Some travel businesses have systems departments of 20, 30 or more people, or a smaller department perhaps supported by the head office of the travel group that owns them. In one of these larger IT departments, says Paul Richer, 'you might get a job as an assistant to a manager if you've done some IT electives and combined those with travel studies in your degree. Small tour operators might not employ anyone systems-wise, but might appoint someone who can help out generally around the office and is good enough at PC and PC applications to help out with the basic IT requirements.' In school leavers, tour operators might be looking for a junior who knows a bit about PCs and PC applications.

DOT.COMS

Not many newcomers to travel are going to set up a travel dot.com company straight away (are you?) ... but as there's been huge publicity about the rise – and projected fall – of dot.coms like lastminute.com, here's a little bit about them.

It's hype, hype, hype, and will continue to be until the whole business settles down. This will take years, because what is happening truly is a revolution. Lastminute.com didn't in fact fail (or hasn't, at the time of writing), though reading the headlines would make you think it had. It is doing reasonable business, adding to its portfolio, and hoping it will increase sales and then hold on when the competition truly clicks in. Airlines and tour operators aren't yet fully geared up to selling direct over the Web. Lastminute.com sell off their late bargains for them. Once they are selling their own – and there are plans for some of the major airlines to come together (despite being competitors) to form their own direct sales website to rival people like lastminute.com – then anything could happen.

And where are the workers in all this? This side of the industry is full of entrepreneurs and technology buffs with some travel people thrown in. A background in travel isn't the first thing you need. As with accountants, lawyers or marketeers, you could just as easily be working in clothing or books or other on-line services, though as Paul Richer says: 'It would help if you've got experience of the travel industry. Those that start without experience find it that much harder.' Paul refers people to a series of articles on the Genesys website about travel and technology, first published in the Travel Trade Gazette. In one of these he talks about five typical qualities in travel e-entrepreneurs: foresight about the Internet and its opportunities, confidence to stick to their beliefs, resolve to overcome financing and other business problems, willingness to take a risk, and motivation:

'Internet entrepreneurs work long days and a weekend off becomes a forgotten concept,' he says.

CALL CENTRES

New technology is also responsible for the huge growth in what used to be called reservations departments, now call centres. As a travel director says: 'Websites create even more calls. It's a factor of e-commerce that you need more call centre people. Customers can't manage the technology, or they want that little bit of extra information that isn't there, and they just ring, all the time.' It'll be a long time before people using the technology – the public as well as middlemen such as travel agents – and those creating it are exactly in line so that websites give precisely what is required and all the traffic goes solely through the Internet (and, soon, digital TV and other media). It'll be a long time, too, before the customer is sufficiently technology-aware to be able to cope.

Many people think it will never happen: 'I don't think people are going to want to move away from talking to travel staff,' says Paul Richer. 'I don't think consumers will abandon wanting to discuss what they are buying; they'll want to explore what they're buying on-screen then call in on the phone. So people in call centres will need good voice skills and good interpersonal skills.' E-travel people need to make the whole business of travel technology accessible to the average person. That hasn't happened yet.

SKILLS YOU'LL NEED

Anyone working in travel needs basic IT skills. Paul Richer explains: 'The whole of travel is very dependent on IT. Wherever you're employed within travel you'll need IT literacy. For example, reps need to use the tour operator's resort system to download manifests, etc.'

Paul gives his view on the skills needed by people coming into travel IT.

● 'School leavers or graduates need a combination of qualifications in both . travel & tourism and IT, but people who want a career in IT in travel probably need to be graduates.'

● 'IT people tend to sit apart from the rest of the world so good interpersonal skills are very important. You've got to talk to users about what they want, tease this out of them and translate their needs so that other people can understand them. These are the typical skills needed by a systems analyst. You need the confidence to ask people to explain things more, to relate it back to them, to be happy to talk.'

● 'The big issue is to get on the experience ladder and work towards the field of specialists. Decide what you want to do: do you want to get into IT/repping, etc? Then get on the ladder. Don't worry about what you get paid.'

'Right across the travel industry it's not easy to find good people with IT skills,' continues Paul. 'I've just taken on a graduate who'd done a dissertation on IT in travel and tourism, which showed her interest. She's comfortable with PCs and the Web and very intelligent.

That combination of intelligence and having done some research into IT and travel made her attractive. Though there aren't normally these opportunities with management consultancies: we prefer using contractors. What was attractive was her dissertation; she brought it in and it showed us her interest in the issues.'

There are many different IT systems within the industry: there are four **CRS** systems used in travel agencies, for instance. All agents need to be able to use at least one of these, and as technology moves on so everyone within the industry will need further skills. Recruiters currently ask for an ability to use a CRS; soon, it will be Internet literacy.

PRACTICAL INSIDER INFORMATION ON HOW TO GET THE JOB

'It might be a case of a good speculative letter,' advises Paul. 'Tour operators might know they want someone but might not want to employ someone specifically for IT. But travel is an IT business and people should always stress their IT confidences: "I'm very comfortable with Word"; "I'm familiar with spreadsheets"; "I can develop basic Web pages".

'Some travel system development companies run graduate training programmes: they "grow their own" because they can't get experienced people. So it's worth approaching these companies. We have a page on our website that lists these companies; there are other links that might be useful.'

GLOSSARY
● **CRS**
Central Reservations Systems. Computer systems used by travel agents to book flights, holidays, and so on.
● **dot.com**
An Internet company.
● **IT**
Information Technology.

USEFUL ADDRESSES
www.genesys.net; search for similar organisations and their links.

FERRY CABIN ASSISTANT

TRAVEL RATING: 7/10, but once you're in a foreign port there will still be work to do, and the boat leaves again soon – perhaps even 20 minutes after docking. There could be concessionary travel such as cheap stand-by airline tickets, free train travel around Europe, and free ferry tickets.

MONEY: Low basic salary usually topped up with shift allowances, probably starting on about £8,000.

HOURS: Shift work and long hours, often extended if there's bad weather or other problems. Blocks of time off in lieu.

HEALTH RISK: 6/10. It's gruelling clearing up everyone else's puke.

PRESSURE RATING: 5/10. If you like dealing with people and enjoy a crisis now and again, then it's a fun job with good teamwork and not too much pressure.

GLAMOUR RATING: 6/10. Snazzy uniform.

Cabin crew? Must be an airline. But all means of transport need customer service staff to look after the passengers. Cabin assistants and managers work on board ferries in a number of different customer-contact roles.

It's a job that pulls together all sorts of skills: the patience, level-headedness and friendliness of anyone in customer service through to languages in some roles, cleaning in others. Some employers would ideally recruit only people with languages, but it can be hard to find and keep good staff. The ferry services have been through a crisis recently owing to the opening of the Channel Tunnel and the loss of duty-free exemption, but things are levelling out; fares have risen significantly, and trade is good. Hopefully this will translate into better pay and working conditions than we've seen recently.

Cabin assistants work with passengers on the many ferries around the UK. The work can include anything from manning the information desk or bureau de change to serving in the shop or answering queries from passing passengers. With some ferry companies it might also include cleaning the boat at the end of the shift (something you might not be told at interview). Your major concern, though, is passenger safety, and you'll be trained to deal with any emergency.

Elaine Robertson works a cross-Channel route as a cabin assistant. She says: 'I really enjoy the job. There's a young person's atmosphere and everyone sticks together, it's fun. But if it runs late you get stuck on the boat for perhaps fifteen hours, with customers complaining.'

Elaine works a shift system which involves getting up before five some mornings, driving to the port already in uniform, and attending the briefing for that sailing. The cabin manager checks that there are enough crew to comply with safety requirements – the boat cannot sail without.

Once on the boat she prepares a muster list of everyone on board and radios and faxes it ashore before handing muster cards to all members of the cabin crew. These state where each person should go in the event of an emergency, and what they should do. Crew need to learn this for each sailing, so that when asked by safety inspectors, or, of course, in case of a real emergency, they know what to do without having to read their card.

Night shifts involve sailing later in the day and returning by approximately midnight, but then being on cleaning duty until the shift ends at six in the morning. But they are quieter sailings, and staff often leave early to make up for the extra hours worked during late day sailings. Elaine also has blocks of free time to make up for the long hours and shift system.

TRAINING

'There are constant drills,' explains Elaine. 'We need to know exactly what to do if the captain sends a coded message over the Tannoy; each person has a section to clear of passengers, and, in case of fire, trained people have fire-fighting duties.' Elaine has also learned the emergency evacuation procedures and practises them repeatedly. She has even jumped down the escape chutes and landed in a life-raft that has been lowered by cranes. As well as this, the intensive initial training included basic sea

survival jumping off high platforms into a cold swimming pool with life-jackets; fire-fighting; first aid at sea; and basic food hygiene – all in separate one-day courses. Then there was a ten-day customer service course followed by work shadowing on board a boat.

PEOPLE ON BOARD

Staff on board include the ship's officers, such as the master, first officer and chief and assistant engineer, and the general operatives, who load the cars and so on. Cabin crew include a cabin manager, senior cabin assistant and then a minimum number of cabin assistants, depending on the safety guidelines of the boat.

SKILLS YOU'LL NEED

'You've got to be determined, accept the hours and conditions and always be flexible,' says Elaine. 'There's a high turnover of people who can't cope with the lifestyle and work in some companies. It does muck up your social life and your family life. It's not ideal for people who've got children.' You'll probably need a language, though it's worth applying even if you haven't got one; also good GCSEs and good communication skills, plus the patience and level-headedness that make you equally effective whether talking to an irate customer or evacuating the craft. Previous customer service experience is also useful, even Saturday shop work or bar work. Some cabin assistants have vocational qualifications and degrees – these are more important if you plan to get into management.

Employers need good, multilingual,

presentable staff, but they rarely stay long: once experienced, ambitious people move up the ladder into more senior roles or, more commonly, on to cruise ships, into airlines or other areas of the travel biz.

PRACTICAL INSIDER INFORMATION ON HOW TO GET THE JOB

Write to the ferry companies; they have recruitment packs that describe the various jobs they have on offer and the skills and experience you'll need. At larger ports they may hold group interviews: the main thing is to be prepared with information about the job and to think beforehand about the type of people they need.

'Find out about things like who does the cleaning,' says Elaine, 'the realities of the hours you have to work, how long it really takes to get promotion, and the average length of time people stay. Some companies are far better than others. But whoever you work for, it's really good experience: you'll get another customer service job easily if you can do this.'

FOREIGN EXCHANGE

TRAVEL RATING: 1/10. This is an office or agency job, though you'll have concessionary travel through working in the travel biz.

MONEY: Standard travel agency pay, usually without a commission element (see Travel Agent section).

HOURS: Standard agency hours or shift work.

HEALTH RISK: 3/10. Rare meetings with masked intruders (which means you are boxed off behind a security screen).

PRESSURE RATING: 4/10. Not too pressured until the queues start building.

GLAMOUR RATING: 1/10. Handling lots of money seems glam to start with, but as time passes all you get from it is dirty hands.

Foreign exchange workers buy and sell foreign currency and traveller's cheques to travellers. This is often within a high-street travel agency, but could be within a business travel agency or at a travel terminal such as an airport or ferry port.

You also advise customers on the currency type they'll need and the best way to take it, and arrange money transfers. It's a lucrative and very competitive business – for your employer. Sadly, however much dosh passes through your hands, your pay stays more or less the same. Travellers pay a commission on the money bought and sold or, increasingly, pay through the variation between the exchange rate for buying the currency and the exchange rate for selling, which are always different.

THE WORK

Penny is a foreign exchange cashier in a travel agency. She works in a separate secure unit at the back of the shop, usually with a colleague beside her, each with their own tills: 'My till has the bare minimum in it,' she explains. 'Spanish, French, and US dollars, plus sterling and US dollar traveller's cheques. The manager's till has Greek, Portuguese and Cypriot. This is for security. We have most of the money in the main safes out the back – that's also a security thing.'

Penny's customers don't always know what they need, and she advises them on the right currency and the best way to take money abroad. 'We have a book to help us identify currencies and notes,' she explains. 'If we're asked to buy currency, we check it in the book and if the notes are in there, we buy them back.'

You have to concentrate on each transaction and be absolutely sure it is correct before you hand the money over. Occasionally customers try to beat the system: 'Some customers give you large amounts of sterling to count and then they try to distract you. It's happened a couple of times, and you find what they've given you is short.

You have to be careful. Also, a lot of people try to buy money without any ID.' Then Penny will explain that they need either a passport or driving licence to identify themselves. 'Sometimes we get people being rude when we tell them we can't buy back their traveller's cheques without ID,' she says. 'And sometimes it feels like we're a bit imprisoned.'

Nicole Benson is a foreign exchange manager with Holiday Hypermarket. Her role includes ordering currencies, making up customer orders, and sending back unwanted currency. She also banks any sterling each day, does spot checks on the tills, counts their contents, and compiles and sends off figures to the currency suppliers and head office. She also trains new staff. 'I did four years' travel sales with two agencies,' she says, 'and four years' foreign exchange with a high-street travel agency. I went into foreign exchange because I was getting fed up in sales. I wanted something different.' This is not unusual: plenty of sales consultants in travel agencies are trained to do foreign exchange and may spend some time at that desk or, like Nicole, make the move more permanent.

Nicole enjoys her work: 'I like the teamwork,' she says. 'I like it because customers know more what they want, though nine times out of ten you still have to sell to them, recommend what to take. We're constantly busy serving customers or with paperwork, and every day is different.'

OTHER LOCATIONS

'Business travel foreign exchange is totally different,' says Nicole. 'The admin there is more like paying the milkman: writing out cheques. The admin here is more like holiday booking. I've been in business travel: I did the foreign exchange for corporate clients, which meant speaking directly to secretaries. That was a lot of phone work and faxes. Here, it's more interesting.'

SKILLS YOU'LL NEED

You must be able to input data, use computer calculations, and able to work with numbers. Foreign exchange workers know that in the French currency, for instance, there is no ten-franc note, so they need to be able to make up amounts without using a ten.

'You need a lot of common sense,' says Penny. 'Some notes, such as US dollars, all look the same. You need to know how to operate the systems, and make sure you don't make mistakes mixing up the different currencies – for instance, Spanish and Portuguese. You need to put the right code into the computer. You also need a lot of patience.'

PRACTICAL INSIDER INFORMATION ON HOW TO GET THE JOB

People usually move into foreign exchange from other roles in agency or business travel work. As Nicole says: 'The college courses are aimed at travel: people don't consider foreign exchange within travel. It's considered an extra product in a travel agency.' You'll probably be trained in foreign exchange if you work for a high-street agency, and be able to take over that role as necessary. Once experienced, you'll be able to move over to a specialist role.

HOLIDAY REPRESENTATIVE

TRAVEL RATING: 8/10. You can work anywhere in the world ... if it's a package holiday destination.

MONEY: The glamour, the chance to travel ... you want to be paid as well? Probably about £350–£450 a month for the months you're being trained or working, plus some or all of your keep. You may get commission on top of this and may do very nicely.

HOURS: Constant. You'll be lucky to see a beach let alone lie on it, except on your day off, when you'll feel it's so important to enjoy yourself you might not.

HEALTH RISK: 5/10. Nothing obvious – more the gradual erosion of sanity.

PRESSURE RATING: 5–10/10. Depends on you. If you love pressure and challenge and being with all sorts of people, you'll thrive.

GLAMOUR RATING: 5–10/10. You may see working abroad as glamorous, but in fact the work can be pretty much a drudge. But you'll get the chance to dress in drag to entertain the guests. Most of the time you'll dress in the company uniform.

A holiday rep? Wow! You've made it – overseas, glamour, clubbing, sunbathing on a golden beach ... Well, not quite. That's the holidaymaker; you're there to work. But for the right person this is the place to be. You'll have a wild time and make a great start to your career in travel. Doranne Reid says: 'And the "right person" can be an unqualified school leaver, a career-break professional or anyone else.' Academic qualifications hardly come into it.

There are many different ways of approaching this job, though the basics are cast in stone: it's a customer service role. Holiday reps meet, greet, inform, organise, pacify, socialise with and sell to the people who come on holiday with their tour operator employers.

Some reps combine working the summer and winter seasons into a virtually full-time job. In the summer, you'll go out to resort in March or April and spend some time training and getting to know the area and its attractions, as well as the people and set-up. Then you'll work the season and come back in late October or November to spend the grey month in the UK. If you can get winter repping work (usually by first building up a track record with an employer) you'll go out to the ski resorts in early or mid-December for the season, which hots up (or cools down) after Christmas. Then back to the UK just in time to get on the plane for the sun ...

It sounds idyllic. And it can be a good career move, too: many people who work in travel started out repping. So whether it is a planned career masterstroke or something that feels right for now, it's undoubtedly excellent training for whatever you end up doing.

THE WORK

The role of the rep is to support people. Your duties could include:

● Transfers – meeting people at airports and delivering them back again at the end of their holiday. (See Transfer Representative section.)

● Welcome meetings. You'll explain everything, from the country's customs to how to buy provisions and what to do about special requirements. You'll explain about cockroaches, excursions (see below), and how to get home at the end of the holiday. Anything.

● Day-to-day visiting of hotels. Most reps visit each hotel or complex most days of the week. You'll have one day off a week, so some tour operators have service centres where customers can always find a rep.

● Organising and booking excursions. Many tour companies pay their reps a basic salary and expect you to top this up with commission on the tours you sell.

● Taking money and dealing with it correctly.

● Filling in forms for health and safety audits and other reporting systems.

● Socialising with the guests.

● You're there for the day-to-day, but also to deal with things when they go wrong. If there's a car crash, or someone needs to go to the clinic or the police station, there are certain officials in resort who will not converse in English, so it's up to you to help the customer.

WHAT'S IT LIKE?

It's hard work. And you commit yourself to a season's work: even if you hate it from day one, you'll have let your flat and sold your car back home. 'I'd recommend it a hundred and fifty per cent,' says Doranne Reid, who now works in the contracts department at Panorama, 'because it gives you a very good insight into another world altogether, and you get paid for it. For people that age, for a few years, it's worth it to be able to live and work in a different country from your own, to get to know about other people's culture and languages.'

It's a much more demanding role now than in the past because of changes to the legal side of things. You have to be into people big style, and if you don't like people, repping's not for you. 'A lot of reps go into it who unfortunately are very preoccupied with themselves,' says Doranne, 'and they don't last. You have to have some understanding of people because you spend so much time looking after them; a lot of that looking after is with unhappy people, long hours, six days a week. You may have three hundred people, but sorting out one couple's problems may take you three hours because of where you are. It can be finding somebody an adapter in a country that doesn't produce them. It can be a death. It's good for you; it's good training and it teaches you not to be selfish. It's incredibly addictive if you're the right sort of person. It depends where you go. I wouldn't rep Club 25 but you get good Club 25 reps who would hate Tunisia – it depends who you are as a person and where you are working.'

Hayley Williams now works as a travel consultant but spent a season in resort, firstly as a kiddie rep, then as a mainstream rep. She remembers her time there: 'I had two hotels to look after. It was such hard work. I've never known people be so rude and nasty. No one deserves to be threatened just because they're a member of a company. I would never do it again. I did that for four months: up at seven, bed at one in the morning because of the paperwork and the tickets and airport drops and welcome meetings. One day I worked from nine a.m. and didn't get back from a transfer until seven a.m. the next day. Then I started work again at nine. The clients are angry and you're tired.

'It was a challenge, and I did enjoy it at times. Before I went out I wasn't very independent, and I'd get upset by complaints at work: I'd cry when people shouted at me. You do develop real customer service skills from it. It's great if you want a challenge, you're outgoing, love people and don't mind working long hours. The nice people were the best; they'd thank you very much at the end of their holiday. I'm glad I did it, even though it was hard work. But I couldn't have done it for another season.'

David West of Panorama sees several different types of people who go repping:

1 People who come in and want to rep for a couple of years, to travel, and to experience a completely different way of life. They like dealing with people but ultimately they are going to do something else. A lot of new graduates want a break before they go into their profession: they may go straight into repping then travel, or the other way around, before settling down into their profession.

2 Others who just want to go overseas to live a different life.

3 The minority, who view it as a career. Perhaps they have no formal qualifications in travel and have decided that it's an area they would like to get into. More and more, though, reps have qualifications – a Leisure & Tourism degree or GNVQ or similar. They've got a good insight into what the industry is all about.

'The first and third types often make excellent reps,' says David. 'They want to have fun, but they still do a professional job. On training courses you can see that these people are going to go out and be star performers. I think all companies will strive to make their reps excellent but, in reality, you get good reps, you get some who you think are hopeless, and then occasional ones who know what the job is all about.'

TRAINING

You'll train in resort before your customers arrive. This means March/April time, and December for the winter season. The training covers both what a rep does, and product knowledge. Joe Lynch works for Neilson and explains how his company organises training for reps: 'At the beginning of each season we go on a one- or two-week training programme where all the overseas troops mass together and have training about public speaking, about presentations, about how to handle complaints and resolve conflict. And then throughout the year there are lots of opportunities for training. Some are out there; some are in the UK; some you do in the winter period: if you're not working the winter you go and do an extra course.' Tracy Turki is an administrator in resort: 'When you first arrive as a new rep you've got to see the country in order to be able to sell it to the guests. So your first couple of weeks is doing the organised excursions and going out and about so that when somebody says "What do you see at Dougga?" you know what it's all about.'

All this won't sink in until you've interacted with the customers – with varying success – over the first weeks and months. But there's always back-up and additional training, and teamwork in resort should be good enough to get you through even the worst of your cock-ups.

SALARY AND ACCOMMODATION

Some people think it's brilliant to be paid for living in the sun and having fun at the same time; others see it differently, as Tracy explains: 'I think people are put off by the conditions and salary because it sounds very low. An average rep will get £350 a month gross. I've got friends who are interviewing people for the travel industry and they say you get some great people, but the moment that you mention salary their faces drop. It can't be a job that you'd do for the money but because you want something completely different, you want to travel, and you want to live abroad.'

Salaries vary, both from one employer to another, and also depending on your job and how much commission you can earn. With **youth products**, the basic salary is low and the commission you get from selling trips and excursions in resorts is high – this balances the salary. With **mainline tour operators** pay is weighted more towards the basic salary, and the commission is a bonus to give the reps pocket money in resort. David West, Panorama's human resources director, recalls: 'There have been programmes on TV where some companies are really pushing trips and the reps are given very tight targets. Their job is dependent on meeting these targets, so it's a very hard sell. It really depends – we as a company have a mixed bag of clients: in some resorts clients want to do things off their own back. Guests are offered excursions to enhance their holiday and the view has always been that the quality of trips should be sufficient that people enjoy them and feel that they do get something for their money. So it depends on the companies.

'Reps' salaries have increased within UK tour operators, over the last few years, to more of a market rate. They get their accommodation and might also have food, in agreement with the hotels.' Andrew Farr, who has spent many years in resort and now works as Panorama's training manager, says: 'You can save £450 a month untouched in your UK bank account repping, as you live free and your wages sit in your bank at home.'

'Their basic salary and their commission,' explains David, 'are on a par with a reasonable salary in the UK or Ireland with people working in a customer service role in catering, hotels, etc. We pay in the region of £425 a month for a first-year representative. In addition, a rep in Majorca will probably only earn £100 per month commission as it's not a place where people will want to go on trips. Somewhere like Tunisia, because there are good trips to go on, or Cyprus, where a trip to Egypt and Israel costs £150, they can earn in excess of £800 per month in commission.'

All companies include accomm-odation. Some have always offered reps their own rooms while others required you to share. That has changed now, along with reps' expectations and what they are willing to accept: people will not share rooms any more. Some companies try not to use hotel rooms but instead use locally rented apartments in residential areas, to give you some quality of life when you finish work. You'll have some food where you're working: breakfast or dinner, perhaps. So adding together your basic salary, commission, accommodation and food, it's not such a bad deal. A first-year rep's package is probably about £12,000, which is on a par with people going into a job in a hotel.

TRAVEL

Some reps will travel for a month or six weeks between seasons. Because you've created relationships and established contacts within the industry (and not just within your own company), you might get a cheap flight to go and stay with a rep from another country, perhaps, or arrange accommodation direct with a supplier. In addition, most tour operators offer concessions to overseas staff. This is an amount of money to use towards holidays, with discounts for your partner.

AGE REQUIREMENTS

There's generally a minimum age of 21 for reps (for children's reps it's 19 or 20, but they need a qualification in childcare – see the relevant section). As David West says: 'If someone can send in an application to demonstrate that they have worked in a service industry, have travelled and perhaps lived overseas, we will invite them in for an interview and assess their maturity because you can get twenty-one-year-olds who are older than twenty-six-year-olds.'

Some tour operators have people working as reps into their late fifties. These more mature people have had a career, or families, and now want to settle overseas. Perhaps their relationship has broken down, and they have gone off to do something they've always wanted to do. One man retired out to Tunisia with his wife. He's an active person and couldn't sit about doing nothing, so he now reps, and loves it. 'They make brilliant reps,' says David. 'They've got so much experience of the world. The customers who go to the small islands or resorts – Madeira, for instance – are well established and are more independent; they want someone they can relate to. It's finding the mix: we need the wild child who will go and party all night and we need people who can relate and talk to other guests and have an interest in opera or whatever.'

BUT ONE DAY IT ALL ENDS

Many people have a wonderful time working abroad for tour operators. Some do just one season while others go back year after year. Few leave in the middle of a season. But very few do it longer term. Joe Lynch explains how he felt: 'A lot of people leave because they get tired of the endless customer contact. They have this dream of a glamorous lifestyle whereas in fact it's bloody hard work, sunrise to sunset plus a bit more. Also, people leave because of the uncertainty: if you're doing seasonal work you're never sure where you're going to be the next season, and some people get tired of the nomadic lifestyle. I could have stayed out there after five seasons but I decided that that was it: it was time to stop. Some people stayed out too long, and the desire to be working all day every day became stale. I was always conscious that if I ever became tired of it, it was time to stop.'

LIFE AFTER REPPING

Plenty of the people who feature in this book started as reps. Once you've done it, you'll have a thorough understanding of the customer end of the travel business. This will take you into work in travel or any of the service industries – tourist boards, local government tourist services, travel agencies, as a tour guide, and, of course, continuing work within tour operations.

There are also plenty of reps who just want to live overseas. 'My idea was to see the world,' says Tracy. 'But I started and stopped in Tunisia.'

SKILLS YOU'LL NEED

If you like people in all shapes and forms and have an outgoing personality, are friendly yet tough, organised and numerate, and maybe have an extra language or two, it's the work for you. As a rep the hours can be 24 hours a day, seven days a week, so you need to be happily dedicated to getting up in the middle of the night, taking transfers at all hours, and being bright and breezy with guests the next day. And always, always punctual. It helps to have an understanding of and a basic conversational level in the local language, though it's not essential.

You need admin skills but, says Joe Lynch, 'overall, it's the ability to get on with people all the time. As soon as you start to lose your energy or enthusiasm for what you're doing it's so apparent, the guests can see straight away.' You don't have to be a life-and-soul type but you do need to be confident, because you're looking after groups of people and presenting to them. People have different styles – some are very brash; others will just chat about what guests might like to do on a particular day.

You don't need specific academic qualifications, though more and more people study for a vocational qualification. Some employers might ask for a certain level of education – perhaps five good GCSEs, including maths, English and a language if possible.

PRACTICAL INSIDER INFORMATION ON HOW TO GET THE JOB

In this section, recruiters talk about the repping recruitment procedure. This applies to mainstream holiday rep work, but elements of it are also relevant to other types of repping. See the individual sections for more specific hints and information on those. Much of it also applies to applying for any job in the travel and other service industries.

TIMING

Although you can apply for a repping job at any time of year (recruiters may keep your details on file if your timing is wrong), it's best to apply in December and January for the summer season. Winter reps need to apply from the end of June to August. It's all but finished by September, although there may be a few vacancies left.

WHAT TO DO

Although many people see it as a tough, underpaid and unglamorous job it's highly sought after, and many companies have found that they don't need to advertise. David West, who recruits for Panorama, explains how he sees it: 'We prefer to get on-spec people who have gone into travel agents and got the brochures, or have seen us in a book for jobs abroad. They want to do the job and have a reasonable understanding of what it's about. Probably three-quarters of the

people we offer to are people who write on spec.'

You can get addresses from brochures, but remember that no one travel agent stocks all the brochures. For a listing write to ABTA, and AITO for the smaller tour operators (see Useful Addresses below). Smaller companies may have a different approach to recruiting, training and employing their reps. That could be something that will suit you better, so it's worth trying a number of different types of organisations.

You can also try the Internet, and the national papers for those tour operators which only sell direct. When positions are advertised, they appear in the broadsheet newspapers and the trade press: *Overseas Jobs Express*, *Travel Trade Gazette* and *Travel Weekly*.

The major employers issue recruitment packs describing the sort of people they are looking for, the qualifications and experience you'll need, and some information about the job itself. It'll also tell you how to apply, and will include an application form. It's worth reading this pack really well, and seeing what hints you can get about the sort of employer they are. For instance, is there much about their commitment to training? Does the information describe the training process at the start of the season and how it is topped up? Does it look at career opportunities? If there is little or no mention of these things it's not necessarily a bad sign, as you can ask at interview, but it's worth having your antennae tuned in right from the start. What other issues are you keen to find out about? And how much do they 'sell' the job to you? Again, a slick sales job doesn't necessarily mean they have anything to hide, but it's worth noting, partly to avoid ending up with a company that doesn't have a good enough product or doesn't support you adequately.

Once you've read, and digested, the literature, you need to work out which companies would suit you best, and take time over your applications.

APPLYING

'There is a very clear instruction to complete the application form,' says David. 'So people who send in application forms that say "see CV" we say no to.' David sends out another form anyway, to encourage them to reapply, but, he says, 'they think they've blown it already. And they probably have. Most people don't bother to fill it in after that.'

Recruiters are looking for people who have worked in the service industry in some way: 'We look for customer care experience,' says David. 'Saturday jobs in shops or bars or hotels or whatever. We also look at where they've travelled and for how long. A lot of people are completely culture-shocked when they've gone overseas.

'Presentation is also very important, and the quality of the writing. There's also a box on the application form for applicants to fill in. Punctuality is on this.' David explains how some people will actually write 'not very good' under punctuality, even though it is vital in

the job. This will be addressed during interview if other elements of the application are good.

YOUR INTERVIEW

The easiest way to watch people interact, and the fastest way of seeing a large number of people, is via the group interview, so this is an industry norm. 'We hope to give as much information as possible in the job specification,' explains David. 'We then interview perhaps seventy per cent of the applications. Using a group interview is an opportunity to include people we might otherwise drop at screening stage. We're not lenient but we like to be fair in our screening process. I always view the application as the first part of the interview and people who send in inferior applications won't be invited. We are looking for people to give us something to make us think: this person is interesting.'

Panorama's group interviews last four to five hours. Staff spend time in the group interviews being very honest about what the job entails. They look at the role and life of the rep and the advantages and disadvantages of the job. They also play up the disadvantages and sideline the advantages of the work, so that you get a more realistic idea of what it's really like. For example, many people are tempted to a life repping because of the wonderful hot weather in resort. 'But what they tend to forget,' says David, 'is that for most of the season it's going to be eighty degrees plus, and they are in full uniform in their tie and jacket, at the airport, working in that environment. Whereas in the UK the country tends to stop if we have a few days of hot weather, they've got it for four months.' Cockroaches are another example: 'We have ants; they have cockroaches. They don't mean it's dirty; they're just everywhere. They'll be in their shoes in the mornings.'

The interviewers then summarise what Panorama is about, and go through case studies where they give examples of situations that a rep could come across, and ask candidates to tell them what they might do. 'We don't look for a right or wrong answer,' David explains. 'What we look for are customer care skills and common sense, the ability to think on their feet without passing the buck. Answers that will diffuse the situation using their communication skills.'

Candidates also do a presentation for three or four minutes, about anything they want. 'We ask them to plan for that and bring along visual aids,' explains David. 'The aim is to assess their preparation and presentation skills. A lot of people come very well prepared. You also get people who are good at ad-libbing and do a better presentation than someone who is nervous.' But which does he prefer? 'We ask that they produce visual aids because we get people who have never done this kind of thing before. Perhaps their presentation is awful, but afterwards we can see that they have got very good notes and visual aids and they have planned it with a good structure. We can train them to do presentations if the rest of their interview is good and shows us

that they have good customer care skills. If someone who hasn't done so well on customer care gets up and ad-libs a very good presentation, we would look at the fact that they haven't planned. We want people who show commitment, people who have sat at home boring their parents for days, even if when they come here it's awful because they're so nervous: if other elements are good we would offer them the job.'

There's also a maths and a grammatical test at the Panorama interview day. The grammar test is because there's a lot of admin in the role of a rep: health and safety audits and customer relations reports that could be used in a court of law. They need people to be able to fill these in professionally, and if you can't spell, or your writing is appalling, they wouldn't be able to use the report. That might lead to the company losing a case in court.

The maths test is to see that you are reasonably financially aware. As a rep, you'll take money for excursions, and refund people for various elements of a trip or holiday they have not had. In some resorts, you could collect £5,000 by the end of a welcome meeting. You're responsible for that, and although obviously if it is stolen from you that's not your fault, if it's lost, or stolen 24 hours after you should have banked it, then you're accountable for the money.

'It's a long day, but we give them lunch,' says David kindly. But – aha! – watch how you eat your spaghetti: 'It's an opportunity for people in the overseas department to come across and chat. It's when people drop their guard and we find out more about them. We might chat to them to try to bring them in more if they're very quiet. Or we might say to people who are obviously not interested that they can leave now, or can stay if they like.

'We follow this through on the day for everybody with one-to-one interviews. We don't spend very long with "nos". We tend to spend longer on those we're not sure about. With a yes, there might be a particular thing that wants addressing, but even at that stage we won't say yes. We do all the nos first, then we do the yeses, then we do all the unsures, when there's more time.'

'We're very nice to them,' says David. 'We pride ourselves on our interviews.' He describes coming back to the UK after working in resort, and starting out in recruitment. He was sent undercover to other companies' recruitment days, to see how they operated. 'In one company,' he remembers, 'after the group interview the recruiters came into the room at the end of the day and called out five names. Those five people were told in front of the remaining people that they weren't successful. That was awful. The rest of us sat there and thought: thank you but no thanks. At another interview day we were given numbers. There were fifty of us and we were called by numbers, never by name; it was awful.'

Procedures like this can tell you a lot about the company, its commitment to its personnel, and how it might be to work there.

How Panorama Decide

'We, and other companies, have criteria that we're looking for.' These include:

● People who have got service skills, and have worked within the service industry.

● Experience of working or living overseas.

● Language skills.

● A qualification in childcare or counselling.

'If an applicant has the other skills but not the languages we would probably offer them the position. It's getting the balance really.

'Some people will come along in a cardi and skirt because of financial constraint, but they still look smart. Others will come along in jeans and T-shirts because their perception of the role is that it's relaxed overseas. Presentation is very important. At the end we might ask why they came in jeans, if they were good in other areas. Unless they'd been stars in the interview we would take that into consideration.'

HOW TO DECIDE WHICH JOB TO TAKE

Larger companies are often able to offer:

● More structured training.

● Larger teams in resort.

● A greater choice of destinations.

● A chance to move within the organisation to different resorts next season.

● More career opportunities back home.

Conversely, they can appear

impersonal, and it can be difficult to get the support you need if the management structure is ineffective.

Smaller organisations have:
● A more personal approach.
● Their training and support can be fantastic or conversely they can be overstretched.

One advantage of a smaller organisation is that they won't stay in business if they give poor client service, and as the person the client sees is the rep, they will probably ensure that you are happy. But equally, they may have more stringent recruitment requirements as there is less back-up in resort for beginners.

There are some great companies and great jobs, and others that would finish off even the most experienced professional. Here's one anecdote from Rosalind Wolfarth, a travel agent: 'I talked to clients who'd been on holiday where the reps had been going to bed and crying every night. The clients were justified in their criticisms of the property, which was terrible, but what could the reps do about it? They weren't getting the back-up from head office. Some of the good companies will give the support they need but with some of the less reputable companies there's no support for their staff, and you feel desperately sorry for them.'

GLOSSARY
● **Mainline tour operators**
Brands like Panorama and Thomson, which offer a general package tour combination where reps look after the guests.
● **Youth products**
Club 18–30, Twenties, etc. – aimed at the younger market.

USEFUL ADDRESSES
● ABTA – Association of British Travel Agents, 55–57 Newman Street, London W1P 4AH. Tel: 020 7637 2444. www.abtanet.com; information@abta.co.uk
Go on-line for a list of all their members (650 tour operators plus over 7,000 travel agencies). Or contact ABTA for shorter listings, e.g. all the tour operators with programmes to Canada. ABTA cannot send out the full listing.
● AITO – Association of Independent Tour Operators, 133a St Margaret's Road, Twickenham TW1 1RG. Tel: 020 8607 9080. www.aito.co.uk; aito@martex.co.uk
These are tour operators which aren't owned by a larger organisation; they tend to be smaller niche operators. Some may also be members of ABTA but you may get new contacts here.

This section has dealt with mainstream repping. There are plenty of other people in resort. See sections on:
● Administrator
● Bar work overseas
● Children's representative
● Instructor
● Resort manager
● Transfer representative
● Winter sports

HOTEL MANAGER

*Perhaps hotels don't spring to mind when you think of the travel business. But travellers have to stay somewhere, and along with apartments, campsites, guest houses, motels and even **botels**, they're big business.*

Hotels are booming. The City now sees the **hospitality industry** as a serious money-making concern. Hotels often belong to large chains, perhaps publicly quoted. A large part of their business, as well as accommodating the traveller from both home and abroad, is in corporate work such as conferences, exhibitions and fairs. They also cater to private functions such as weddings. All of this needs a strategy and careful and on-going planning: it's not just a matter of cleaning the bedrooms and stopping the chef serving rat soup the day he jacks it all in. It's a complex business, and similar in lots of ways to other work in this book as it, too, is a service industry. Many of the skills required by people in hotels are common to others in travel.

Lots of people work in hotels on the way to somewhere else, both literally and career-wise. Many thousands of people have used basic hotel work as a means of travelling around the world: busy cities and resorts will always need casual labour. As far as careers go, Giles Paul, who manages the Belgrave, a 61-bedroom hotel in Brighton, is a good example: he studied for a Higher National Diploma (HND) in Hotel and Catering Management. Of the 120 who started with him, only 60 qualified and now, 23 years on, only two are hotel managers. But plenty more have moved on to other areas of hospitality, travel and elsewhere.

There are many roles in a hotel behind the scenes – all the kitchen work, **housekeeping**, accounts and administration, for instance. Hotel managers usually work their way up through **front-of-house**, though. They are people who want to interact with others and give guests a good experience, sort out any problems, and who thrive on the buzz of being out there. 'It's something that has to be in the blood,' says Giles. 'It's not a nine-to-five job. You could work twenty-four hours a day, seven days a week. When you're learning, you don't necessarily get the pay for any extra hours but you get the experience to progress. You've got to enjoy it.'

Giles started in hotels at fourteen, working as night porter and kitchen porter in the school holidays. 'They were menial jobs, but great fun. I've always enjoyed every aspect of what I do.' After more part-time experience and then an HND, with two six-month placements, he started working full-time in a variety of lowly roles as part of a management training scheme. Moving hotels every two or three years, which you need to do if you are building a career, he was appointed a night manager. 'This is the route into front-of-house management, because you have exposure of running all aspects of the hotel, in all areas, from nine p.m. to eight a.m. Then I would stay on longer in the daytime to help out and get more experience. I've always been a bit of a workaholic.'

Most problems end up at the front desk, which is where guests go in the first instance. 'I like mopping up the problems,' says Giles. 'It requires a lot more skill than you first see. It's a pure customer relations situation. You do become an expert at it.' It's very hard work on a reception desk: you may

need to be doing several things at once, and not let it get to you. 'It's mentally demanding: you have to be sharp,' says Giles. 'You've got to like noise and busyness. And it's physically demanding too.'

From his first night management position, Giles went on to an assistant front-of-house management position. His new boss quit after a month and left him running the whole front-of-house operation until a replacement was found. 'I was also a duty manager, one of several who would run the whole hotel when necessary, as well as my own area. Some areas, such as the kitchens, don't have a manager on duty at all times, just when it's busy, so the duty manager assumes control.'

Then he moved to the same position at an 800-bed hotel, then on to become a senior manager with a Brighton hotel, looking after front-of-house, housekeeping, reservations, and also controlling the duty management. He reported to the deputy general manager and the general manager. 'I enjoyed it so much that I stayed seven years,' he says. 'The entire senior management team was there for six years, which is very unusual in hotel management.'

What he enjoyed most was the customers. 'Money doesn't motivate me at all,' he says. 'There's a satisfaction of working with someone for several weeks before a conference or wedding, seeing them have a good time, and then getting the thanks afterwards. The buzz that gives you is what makes it all worthwhile.'

During that time he was offered a great job in a London hotel but turned it down: 'There comes a point when, despite being career-driven, you become less mobile.' He decided to stay in Brighton, and while considering his next move was approached to take on the redevelopment, opening and running of the new Belgrave Hotel, a derelict and, to the council, embarrassing building in a prime seafront location.

He was given more or less free rein to achieve his vision within a new four-star hotel. His aim was to make the Belgrave more modern with a more relaxed feel, an independent haven without a corporate atmosphere, while still maintaining four-star standards. He spends more of his time locked in an office now, though not by choice. But he recognises that 'the time I spent as a hall porter has stood me in good stead for now. I still have to do these things sometimes. If someone doesn't turn up for work, it's a needs-must situation: I made beds here last week. You're never allowed to forget where you come from.'

SKILLS YOU NEED

● Motivation: 'I want people who want to get on, who don't just do the minimum,' says Giles.

● Initiative. Giles is looking for people who don't want to be managed too closely because there isn't always time to supervise a member of staff. Larger hotels and chains are more regimented, with more paperwork and set ways of doing things, but, as Giles says: 'At the end of the day, there's not a rule book for every situation. It's about managing on your feet.'

● You also need to be thick-skinned and not take things personally, and able to leave work behind at the end of the shift. 'As you get older, you tend to get less tolerant,' reflects Giles. 'That's one of the reasons the industry attracts younger people.'

● Languages help. Training schemes don't insist on them, but it will help you get selected if you have one or more foreign languages.

● Multi-skilling: Giles employs people who will work in all areas. It gives people greater job satisfaction, he says. Larger and more traditional hotels might not operate this way.

● 'Experience and qualifications are secondary (unless you're talking about somebody like a chef) because skills can be taught,' Giles says.

PRACTICAL INSIDER INFORMATION ON HOW TO GET THE JOB

There are many ways into the industry but Giles suggests that you do a related course, such as a sandwich course that includes work experience. 'But still do as much related work as possible. The best way to learn is through experience. College without experience is not a good way in. The more hands-on experience you can get in different types of hospitality and catering, anything like a pub, a burger bar, a hotel, the better it will be for you.'

Some people go on to structured management training schemes with large hotel groups while others go less formally into an independent hotel and start to learn on the job, then progress when they're ready.

When Giles is recruiting, he's looking for personality, personality and personality. He wants people who are naturally friendly and customer-focused, and he can only tell by talking to them. 'It's almost a body chemistry thing. I can usually tell within five minutes of the start of an interview if someone is going to make it here.'

As openings in hotels are coming up all the time, make blanket applications, even for positions you don't particularly fancy. 'Don't limit your options. All experience is good experience, and you don't know if you're going to enjoy it until you've done it. You can transfer within the industry quite easily. It's all about being on the inside rather than on the outside. We consider people from within first.'

Giles also recommends that you:
● Write your CV carefully and keep it short, a maximum of two pages. Extras such as testimonials just get in the way: he doesn't have time to read them, and will take up references later if he employs you. Include a précis of all relevant experience, including positions of responsibility in clubs, etc. while at school or college.
● Be on time for your interview. If people turn up late for work it has huge ramifications for the hotel's operations: you can't work flexitime. Showing you're punctual is essential.
● Dress smartly, with at least a jacket and tie for men and equivalent for women. When people turn up scruffily dressed, Giles says: 'We might still interview them, but the decision's already been made. It astounds me how many youngsters turn up in a horrendous state.'

GLOSSARY
● **Botel**
A floating hotel firmly moored in calm waters.
● **Front-of-house**
Looking after reception, checking guests in and out, dealing with all booking requirements, supervising the concierge and the porters, luggage, messages and housekeeping.
● **Hospitality industry**
All the work that goes on to entertain, feed and accommodate people, in hotels, guest houses, bars, restaurants, and so on. Hoteliers might see themselves more in hospitality and tourism than in travel, but there are vast overlaps.
● **Housekeeping**
Cleaning of bedrooms and public areas, control of linen, and so on.

INSTRUCTOR

Suntanned sailors or piste-whizzing demigods; there's a place in each of our fantasies for one of those ... But what's it like to be one?

You could call instructors the 'activity reps'. They represent activity holiday companies overseas, spending most of their time teaching the activities they specialise in. But they're also part of the general resort team and do their share of other work such as transfers and entertaining. The set-up varies from company to company, and you could end up doing anything!

Activity holidays are becoming more and more popular, so there is increasing demand for instructors. A good parallel is to think about ski holidays 25 years ago. Then it was a specialist market: you had to be a good skier, know where to go, and be able to walk up mountains carrying your skis. Now everybody knows that if you want to go skiing you book a skiing holiday. The same is true of other activity holidays; people have realised that if you want to go sailing there are many companies that offer learn-to-sail holidays. You can book one just as easily as you can any other beach holiday and come back an experienced sailor.

THE WORK

Joe Lynch works for Neilson Activity Holidays. He got his first job with them as a sailing instructor in Greece when he left college. 'It was brilliant, I absolutely loved it,' he remembers. 'I liked working outdoors in the sunshine and I liked teaching people sailing and windsurfing. I loved going to work without any shoes on.' As well as instructing he did other work with customers between ten o'clock in the morning and five in the evening, five days a week. After that there were social activities with the customers. 'There is a lot of time with people,' he says. 'It's nowhere near nine-to-five.' As well as instructing and socialising, he'd go to the airport one day a week. 'Nobody can afford just to employ instructors – it's made clear that it's part of it, but I enjoyed that part of the job.'

TRAINING

Although you're already a qualified instructor before you apply, a lot of the training is skills-based to ensure that your current technical skills are maintained, and new ones added. This could mean honing your sailing skills if you are a dinghy instructor, for instance. There's also training in the basics of being a rep, covering customer care and health and safety aspects, and so on. 'At the beginning of each season we'd go on a one- or two-week training programme,' Joe says, 'where all the overseas troops mass together and you have training in public speaking, presentations, how to handle complaints and resolve conflict.'

TIMETABLE

You go out for a full season (April–October) or a temporary season (peak time only). Winter season staff (skiing) go out early December to April. 'This opens up the opportunity to do summer seasons with winter seasons, which I did for two years,' says Joe. 'The synergy between the seasons gives you a month off then back to work again – people come home and stay with parents or friends and relax for November.'

Joe moved resorts for his second season and worked, this time, as a windsurfing senior. The following two summers he worked as a centre manager, responsible for the running of the centre: tuition, transfers, accommodation, staff and customers. Then, in his final year, he was an area manager, responsible for two resorts and the flotilla. But there's a broad base of instructors and only a few area managers, and as most people want to go down that career route opportunities are limited. 'The reason I stopped in the end,' Joe recalls, 'is that I'd done it for four or five years and I thought it was time to unpack.'

SKILLS YOU'LL NEED

People skills: the same as for a holiday rep (see that section). 'As soon as you start to lose your energy or enthusiasm for what you're doing,' says Joe, 'the guests can see straight away.' You also need to be confident because you'll be looking after groups of people, presenting to them and teaching them. 'People have different styles – some are very brash; others will just chat about what to do today. It's up to you.'

As well as these skills you need the core skills of the activity you're teaching, and must be qualified as an instructor. See individual companies' recruitment packs for details, and contact the training association for your sport (addresses below).

'In my experience there is no such thing as a typical member of staff,' says Joe. 'A lot are school leavers who have just got a couple of exams and a windsurfer's qualification; others are college leavers who don't really know what they want to do, who want to try something fun. Others are on career breaks: we have teachers, doctors and veterinary surgeons who just want to get out for a couple of years. We had one lady in her late forties or early fifties who used to come out every summer. People tend to be from a younger age group because of the costs and the salary: they're people who haven't got mortgages. But a lot of people just have a break for two years and work on the yacht or on the beach. It's a bit of a myth that everybody has got to be eighteen years old. It improves the quality of the holidays, too, having people with a bit more life experience.'

PRACTICAL INSIDER INFORMATION ON HOW TO GET THE JOB

'Most people apply to several companies,' says Joe, 'and if you have the right qualifications very often you can pick and choose: there are enough instructors to go around, but if you have a broad base of skills then you are in demand. Female activity instructors are always in demand – there are far more males qualified at the moment.

'Most companies have a recruitment pack that outlines their values and their commitment to training and staff welfare. It's the sort of thing to find out at the interview stage.'

USEFUL ADDRESSES
● The British Association of Snowsport Instructors (BASI), Aviemore, Inverness-shire, Scotland PH22 1QU. Tel: 01479 861717. basi@basi.org.uk
● Professional Association of Diving Instructors (PADI), www.padi.com PADI is international, with service offices in Australia, Canada, Switzerland, Japan, Norway, Sweden, the United Kingdom and the United States – go to their website for contact details.
● Royal Yachting Association (RYA),

RYA House, Romsey Road, Eastleigh, Hampshire SO50 9YA. Tel: 023 8062 7400. admin@rya.org.uk; www.rya.org.uk
See also Winter Sports.

MANAGING DIRECTOR

The managing director (MD) looks after and directs a company: in travel, that might mean a tour operator, chain of travel agents, hypermarket, airline, cruise line, or whatever. It could also mean any small operation that trades as a company.

Businesses need managing. Experienced travel people, or outsiders with experience of running other businesses, head up travel organisations and are often known as managing directors. The businesses they run could be of almost any size. One managing director, Rosalind Wolfarth, owns and runs an independent travel agency. She says: 'I am the managing director but I am just one of the people who work here as far as everyone is concerned. The staff are travel consultants. Our part-time person does the admin and I do some too. We're too small to have defined roles: we all make the tea and coffee.'

An example of a larger-scale business is the tour operator Panorama Holiday Group, built up by Justin Fleming, MD, and Nick Munday, deputy MD. Justin started the business and Nick joined him after eighteen months. Justin's management role grew from having just one member of staff initially to employing two hundred twelve years later. They sold the company to Airtours plc eighteen months ago. 'I'm still MD,' says Justin, 'and we are on target this year to carry 330,000 passengers. We employ about three hundred staff here and abroad, with a separate operation in Dublin with fifty staff.' Justin's main roles now include liaising with the parent company, overseeing the Dublin operation, and **contracting** in Tunisia. The day-to-day running of the rest of the business is Nick's responsibility. This includes finance, technology (there is no IT director), the whole of the marketing, product and sales side, commercial (which is pricing and yield management), human resources, and the overseas operation.

Nick has no day-to-day responsibility apart from managing those divisions: 'There's nothing that falls on my desk that is my work to do,' he says, 'so I am a pure managing director. I shed all of my day-to-day work to relevant people within the structure. I manage the directors and make sure that the strategy of the business stays on track as the board has decided, and I help the directors with their decisions.'

Nick believes that the job of the MD is to ensure that the balance in the business stays with the key levers and drivers for the company. 'If the MD was a totally finance oriented person,' he says, 'all he would be interested in would be the financial side of the business, but that would be wrong because this isn't a finance company. My style of running the business is leadership by example. I run it here by being very much in touch with what the other directors are doing and trying to make constructive comments to help them do their job better.'

This means that Nick needs an understanding of every aspect of the business. This is not easy, especially in a company of Panorama's size, and in travel, a particularly complex industry. 'You need an incredible knowledge of any particular subject to have any bearing on the decision that's being made.' Nick explains how he might start his day in a finance meeting: 'It might be about something complicated about budgeting or some statistical output. Then I might go

straight to a marketing meeting talking about e-commerce, then on to a meeting about a new EU labour law that's affecting personnel recruitment.

'Being an MD is a skill in itself,' he says. 'We don't have an "ivory tower" mentality in this company, as it's grown up from a small business.'

Nick feels that running any business as an MD is a war of attrition, making sure that you never miss a trick, and are better than your competitors. 'I try to have a finger on the pulse of what is going on,' he says, 'and continually work to make the business better. A lot of people will say that's getting too involved at management level but that is my style. This is a very high-risk business that runs on wafer-thin margins, so attention to detail is essential.'

SKILLS YOU'LL NEED

'I'm fairly unique in that I've had an all-round grounding in this industry and this business,' says Nick Munday. As well as that, and in common with many other MDs, he trained as an accountant. 'People with an accountancy training generally have a broad business training which is ideal for running a company. They are also cautious by nature which is attractive to investors. So that's why accountants seem to be running the world at the moment.'

Ambition is important, too. 'I always wanted to run my own business in the leisure industry, from the age of seventeen,' says Nick. 'Before that, I was an entrepreneur: I traded shares from the age of fourteen. I had any number of activities going on: I'd sell strawberries on the beach, do car cleaning, gardening – anything you can think of that made money. I had a burning ambition to run my own business. I wanted to be in control of my own destiny. At fourteen I told everyone that I would be a millionaire and retired by the time I was thirty. I didn't make it, unfortunately.' Most people would say that missing his financial target by a mere decade isn't doing so badly.

PRACTICAL INSIDER INFORMATION ON HOW TO GET THE JOB

It's not a job you'll walk into without a great deal of experience. Don't waste everyone's time trying. But as you work in various roles in travel, watch how the businesses are run and note the skills of the people who run them. If you work to develop the necessary skills and experience, one day it could be you.

Some people spend a year studying for a postgraduate MBA (Master of Business Administration). You can also do this part-time over a longer period. This aims to provide the skills necessary to manage a business, as far as anyone can in an academic setting. Equally important, for many people, are the like-minded students and members of faculty you will meet, many of whom will be interested in becoming entrepreneurs. Even if you never set up your own business, the contacts you make may be invaluable in getting work at this level in the future.

GLOSSARY
● **Contracting**
When a tour operator arranges to rent accommodation – see the separate section.

PILOT

This is the person who sits up front in an aircraft and drives you to your destination.

If you think of working in travel, one of the first images that pops into your head could well be yourself on the flight deck of a jet, flying long-haul to exotic destinations. This becomes, and remains, some people's career aspiration, and as Daniel, a senior co-pilot with a major airline, says: why not? 'There is no institution that advises people to become pilots because there are enough keen people already. That means it's not a standard career that advisers and schools tell you about. But if you're very keen and reasonably intelligent, you'll get in.

'Most pilots love their job,' continues Daniel. 'Most people find it very challenging and very hard work. A fair proportion of pilots are aviators through and through and are obsessed with it, though I'm not. But we all get a thrill through take-off and landing, a big adrenalin rush: you're doing your job to the best of your ability; you have an awesome, massive responsibility, and all in a big shiny aircraft.'

Once qualified to fly jets you'll start as a first officer, one of the two pilots on the flight deck (there are two pilots to ensure that the flight is conducted safely). One will often fly outbound and the other inbound, with the non-flying pilot monitoring everything. Captains are in charge of the aircraft and make the decisions but both pilots have the same technical knowledge and ability.

The trouble with flying long-haul, though, is that there isn't always enough to do. 'There are times,' says Daniel, 'when you're droning away through the night and think: God, I hate this; it's so boring. You could have twelve or thirteen hours on autopilot, reading the paper, but there's only so long you can read a paper for.' Once at your long-haul destination you get two days off, then fly back. 'You're up at night,' says Daniel, 'then stuck in a hotel and asleep during the day. These are the downsides. But there are good things too. For instance, you might go to Cape Town for four days.'

Short-haul tends to consist of five- or six-day trips. On one trip you might fly from London to Rome, back to London, then to Lisbon, all in one day. Then you'd spend the night in Lisbon and carry on from there. At the end you'd get two days off. 'It's actually much harder than long-haul,' says Daniel, 'as you're stopping and starting all the time. It's very different, much more frenetic.'

Daniel also talks about the way the airlines are pushing pilots to think and act more commercially. 'This is central to the job now. Everything is cost-driven. Everyone in the industry must be aware of the commercial aspects and of cost-saving. When I started, safety was everything, but now it's split equally between commercial aspects and safety. You're almost always working. There's a legal minimum number of days off we have to have, and we're often on that legal minimum. There are also maximum legal flying hours. The airline might occasionally push you to exceed these, but if you do you get grounded for a month.

'It is perceived as glamorous,' agrees Daniel, 'both by pilots and outsiders. It makes you think: do I want a nine-to-five job commuting in by train every day? Most people have ten or fifteen years of thinking, Christ, this is fun, before feelings of frustration set in. But this is probably the same with any job.'

DANIEL'S CAREER

Daniel got into flying late, aged 23. He went to a private flying school and gained his licence there, then became an instructor. He paid for all this himself. Then he flew turboprops for a year, to get the required number of flying hours. 'These are aircraft with jet engines powering propellers,' he says. 'They're usually small airline aircraft. They're not used so much now. Nowadays, people would probably go straight on from small aircraft to jets. All pilots want to fly big jets. It's more fun, better money, prestige and all that.'

After gaining the airline-required 500 hours on turboprops he joined a major charter airline and they sponsored him through his **Airline Transport Pilot's Licence (ATPL)**. Daniel now works for a major scheduled airline as a co-pilot, flying 747s.

TRAINING OPTIONS

Until you gain your ATPL you can't join an airline as a pilot. There are three different ways you can get this, unless Daddy's paying, in which case there are four:

1 Train with the forces: the army, air force and navy all train pilots. Here you can fly different types of aircraft, but the airlines prefer ex-forces people who have flown transport aircraft. 'It's broadly the easiest way to get into flying,' says Daniel. 'But all airlines have a non-merit-based seniority system, so when you leave the air force you'll join on less money and less seniority than someone who has trained with the airline. With the air force, you also have to learn to kill people, which not everyone wants to

do.' You can also learn to fly helicopters through the Army Air Corps.

Lindy Simmons, who recruits pilots for Virgin Atlantic, comments that this is 'some of the finest training in the world'. Around half their pilots come through this route.

2 Apply direct to the airlines. If they are recruiting and you are successful, they will sponsor you through your training. It takes about three years to complete the ground and flying school before being let loose on the public. It costs the airline about half a million pounds to train you.

3 'Pay for your training yourself, as I did,' says Daniel. First, obtain your private pilot's licence by joining a flying club and having lessons with an instructor. Then become an instructor yourself, as this is the only way for most people to afford enough flying hours. You then build up your hours and take the appropriate exams. It might take five years to build the hours for the **Basic Commercial Pilot's Licence (BCPL)**, which you need for any commercial work. You could do this with air taxi work. Alternatively, many people go to the United States and build their hours there, as it's much cheaper and the weather's better. But it will still be necessary to take the exams in the UK if you want to work here. Doing it on your own is expensive, probably £15,000–25,000 minimum. 'It's all to do with building flying hours,' says Daniel. 'You can also build these through gliding, flying helicopters, etc.'

4 If you're unhealthily wealthy, you can take an intensive approved

course, spending about a year and upwards of £60,000 on your training. This then qualifies you to fly for a 'third level' airline, a small airline with small planes. With average experience you'll clock up 600–700 hours of flying time a year, so it will take you perhaps five years to gain the 2,500 hours of flying time that you need to fly heavy jets. You may fly larger aircraft of a 'second level' in the meantime, doing short-haul, perhaps, for a charter airline.

FURTHER TRAINING
Commercial factors are increasingly important in the life of a pilot these days, but that doesn't mean safety has declined. You'll receive on-going training and testing at regular intervals – for example, two days of tests on a simulator every six months.

HOW THE AIRLINES STRUCTURE THEIR PILOTS' WORKING HOURS
'There are two different ways that airlines administer the routes that pilots fly,' says Daniel. 'The first system is called bid-line. The junior pilots get all the rubbish because the senior ones choose first. You're paid according to the length of your flight and your destination, with a basic salary based on your length of service. For instance, if I fly to Delhi or Bombay, which is a nine-hour flight and a four-day trip, I get my basic plus about £150. This is made up of £7 per hour up to the first seven hours, then £50 for the next hour, £65 the one after that, then it increases exponentially. If you fly to Buenos Aires, the same

length trip but fourteen hours' flying time, you get £1,400 on top of your basic. So everyone wants to do the long flights. I'm a middle-seniority co-pilot, so I do a lot of the long flights, and I almost double my pay.'

The pilots all have to do the same number of hours flying a month. This means that if you fly to Buenos Aires you can complete a month's work in three trips. But junior pilots don't get to fly there, so they get fewer days off and are paid about half. Even experienced pilots find drawbacks to this system: 'If I go sick I can lose up to £1,400, so sickness rates are very low for longer trips. It's actually illegal to fly when you're unfit, though people sometimes do.'

Other airlines have a rostering system. Here, people in the office decide which flights everyone flies. 'This is terrible,' says Daniel, 'because some person in an office decides where you will fly. It's subject to massive corruption: gifts and money change hands. The bid system is far better, though it's not entirely fair either.'

PAY AND CAREER PROGRESSION

Salaries start at about £18,000 for qualified pilots trained by a major airline. After the first four years, with basic and extras, that rises to just under £30,000. After ten years the pay is about £65,000, which is the ceiling for a first officer. The top scales for a senior captain are about £140,000.

Because of the seniority system within airlines, it can take a very long time to get to the top. There may be a certain number of hours you need to fly before you gain promotion. For instance, captains need a minimum of 6,000 hours with Virgin Atlantic, though it can be less with other airlines. To make captain can take between two and 20 years to achieve at Virgin.

SKILLS YOU'LL NEED

'We have the opportunity to destroy a company,' says Daniel. 'A crash can cost the company one or two billion pounds and the insurers another three billion. Any one of us can do that. So they cannot afford to have low-calibre pilots.'

You'll need the basic five GCSEs at grade C or above and A levels (maths and physics are good subjects), then a degree. As Daniel puts it: 'You're less likely to be accepted with an English literature degree because flying's a technical subject.'

He talks about the other elements that make a good pilot: 'There are skills required that are not academically based. You need to be able to cope with a huge workload under pressure. People who make good pilots come from all walks of life, all backgrounds. We do recruit almost exclusively graduates, though, as they tend to have less trouble with the technical side, but the best pilots are not always from university.'

You'll need team skills, known as Crew Resource Management (CRM). 'It's an integral part of gaining the licence,' says Daniel, 'and is about getting on with the co-pilot and cabin crew. Historically, co-pilots didn't say much and pilots were overbearing, but that's changed now.' You also need delegation skills and to be able to take responsibility. If you can't you're not going to enjoy flying. You mustn't have tunnel vision.

Daniel also comments on an aspect that you might not otherwise consider: 'You need a very good grasp of the commercial market and an understanding of the airline business. I can't overemphasise this: it makes the difference between getting a job and not. At my interview, an airline was in trouble and I was asked what would happen to it. What I said did happen several months later. If all your thinking is about flying, you need to remember that in the air force you're primarily an officer, and in an airline it's primarily the commercial aspect. You must also be above average all your working career, and never make that big mistake. So the degree of professionalism is sky high.'

Daniel feels that it's harder to train as a doctor than a pilot: 'It requires more intellectual skills,' he says. 'A pilot requires fewer academic skills and intellectual ability is less important, but some people can handle it and some can't, regardless of intellect.'

PRACTICAL INSIDER INFORMATION ON HOW TO GET THE JOB

Some airlines, such as Virgin Atlantic, only take pilots with over 2,500 hours' flying experience, which effectively means that they only recruit from the forces or from charter airlines. Others, such as British Airways (which employs over half the pilots in the UK), recruit trainees at certain times and at others follow the same recruitment policy as Virgin.

Even though they prefer graduates, the best way to get training with an airline is to apply direct about a year before you do your A levels. Most of the interview processes take six months to a year. There are all sorts of tests – for teamworking ability, handling on a simulator, reaction times, and so on. 'We're unlikely to take people before a degree,' says Daniel. 'It's safer for us to take graduates. But the later you apply, the less likely you are to get a job. At interview you'll be asked: what have you done about it already? You need to tell them about your flying experience, how you have been following the industry, and so on. The later you think about it as a career, the less chance you have of convincing them. Interviewers are often pilots and recognise the keen ones. Plenty of young men and women are dead keen. The airlines can afford to be choosy.'

When recruiting, the airlines go first for people with the full ATPL, and a type rating, i.e. a licence endorsement for a specific aircraft type, say B737 or B757. Then they go for people with just a flying licence, and after that they look at people with no licence. So the more flying experience you have, the better. Most who are taken on have done some private flying.

Daniel advises: 'If you want to join an airline, spend as much time looking into the commercial aspects as into aviation and you're much more likely to get a job. And if you can, join the

ATC – Air Training Corps – through school or university. It's free and gives you up to thirty flying hours, which would normally cost £30 an hour. By doing this you will find out about the business.'

FURTHER RESEARCH

'The motivation has to come from you,' says Daniel. 'Most pilots talk to pilots; they meet them at flying schools. Instructors at flying schools are building up flying hours and are generally very keen to become commercial pilots. They're the best people to talk to about the business: they have the current knowledge.'

Get hold of the required information from the Civil Aviation Authority at Gatwick (but distributed separately – see below). Ask for the book of requirements for the Airline Transport Pilot's Licence. 'Read it, understand a bit of it (you won't understand it all),' says Daniel, 'and get a pilot to explain it to you. There are other publications for other licences. These lay out the legal requirements. They are all called "CAP" [Civil Aviation Publication] and then a number.'

GLOSSARY

● **Airline Transport Pilot's Licence (ATPL)**
The licence you require to work for an airline.
● **Basic Commercial Pilot's Licence (BCPL)**
The licence you require to do any commercial work at all.

USEFUL ADDRESSES

The two main organisations are:
● AOPA – Aircraft Owners and Pilots Association. Tel: 020 7834 5631. www.aopa.co.uk. All general regulations and information on becoming an instructor. Publishes a free electronic newsletter that you may find interesting.
● CAA – Civil Aviation Authority. Tel: 01293 567171. www.caa.co.uk. Responsible for safety, economic regulation and consumer protection in the aviation industry in the UK. The CAA's CAP booklets on licence requirements are distributed by Westwood Documedia. Tel: 01242 283100. See their catalogue on-line at www.documedia.co.uk
Try the chat room at http://home.ease.lsoft.com/archives/pilot.html

TRADE MAGAZINES

● *Flight International*
The bible for commercial pilots.
● *Pilot*
The private pilots' magazine, for people who pay for their own training.

PRODUCT MANAGER

TRAVEL RATING: 6/10. If your product is overseas you go out to research and monitor, meet the people, and look for new products and markets.

MONEY: Corporate scales, probably about £20,000–£25,000.

HOURS: Office hours plus, with travel as necessary.

HEALTH RISK: 1/10 – varied, interesting work and plenty of sunshine.

PRESSURE RATING: 5/10, unless your product fails.

GLAMOUR RATING: 6/10. It's a back-room job; most people won't understand what you do, there's no pretty uniform, but the travel ups the rating.

Product managers work for travel organisations nurturing particular products, which could be a certain destination such as the Far East or Brazil, or a type of holiday such as World Cup packages, or a certain brand of ticket that appeals to a particular type of traveller, or anything else. It's a **marketing** *role, but all sorts of other processes can be included in it.*

Product managers in most industries have done the traditional career climb, probably through sales or **market research** into marketing support, then promotion up to manager. Travel, as usual, has rules of its own: it may happen this way but equally, if you're ambitious, you can get there via working in resort, agency, ticketing, or wherever. You'll really understand the business if you've worked your way up this way – and you'll understand your product better than a newcomer to the travel business ever will.

Joe Lynch is a product manager for Neilson Active Holidays, looking after all their holidays except skiing. 'I'm responsible for the product marketing: brochure production, the Internet, direct mail campaigns, newsletters, and so on. We go to shows as well. I'm also responsible for ensuring that the product we sell is matching what people are asking for. It's up to me to spot a demand in windsurfing in a different country, for instance, and see if we can get there.'

He started his career in resort as an instructor, then moved into resort management. When he came back to the UK he didn't have any job offers. 'Just for that period it felt like a leap into the dark. I was mostly interested in travel but if not, after five years' experience of looking after people, I'm sure I could have found something in the service industry.'

He'd worked for Neilson in resort, 'but I didn't come straight back to this office. I went to a company organising school and study trips in areas such as history, art, sports tours, science tours, etc. I worked in their educational travel department for two years. That was office-based, booking hotels, coaches and venues, and selling packages to school groups. I occasionally went into the schools. My job title was educational tours manager, which was a product manager really: I looked after that whole product.

'It was very interesting, and something quite new for me. I learned an awful lot generally, like the art history of Paris: you work out which museums are where, and which pictures they have, so you can then talk knowledgeably with an art teacher and get some credibility that way.'

Joe gained the experience he needed to return to Neilson: 'This opportunity came up here, with a company I had a lot of history with, and also it's a product that's my passion: the sailing, windsurfing and ski side of things. I can talk more confidently and more enthusiastically about windsurfing than I can about art in Paris.'

That said, marketing people need to be able to switch between products as the work and organisation dictates. 'You could get a whole roomful of product managers and they would probably give you completely different job descriptions. Essentially, it's tailoring the product to fit the market, a marketing-type role.'

Product managers in this industry need first-hand experience of their product and the people who deliver it. 'I travel quite a bit because before you can talk about a hotel you need to go and see it – you have quite a lot of resort visits.' There's also market research to undertake or commission, feedback from other departments to analyse, and product development geared to the company's overall plans. You'll probably report to the marketing director, who has overall control of the 'sharp end' of the business (see Sales and Marketing section).

And overall? 'I love it,' says Joe. 'It's very exciting, you never know what's coming next. It's always busy; you're always looking for new opportunities with promotions, or new destinations.'

SKILLS YOU'LL NEED

If you're going the academic route you need good GCSEs, some A levels and maybe a business-related degree. Otherwise, you'll be able to pick up the marketing expertise as you get into the role, but you do need to be an outgoing type, to like people, have an analytical mind, and a certain toughness. But you'll have all these anyway if you're an ambitious travel person. And, as Joe says: 'You also need to get into the frame of mind where if someone says "Can you go to Spain tomorrow?" you say "Yes, I can do that".' Somebody who's not used to travel may need a week's notice and all sorts of planning.

PRACTICAL INSIDER INFORMATION ON HOW TO GET THE JOB

If you're working your way up, then you'll get the feel for the type of person who's successful and try to move in the appropriate direction. Do your time at the bottom; show you're good, and apply for internal positions when they come up. If you're coming in as a marketing person there are the usual sources of vacancy ads: the trade and marketing press, word of mouth, and so on.

GLOSSARY
● **Market research**
Finding out how well the product is

liked, or might be liked if it's a new product being developed, by asking the people who use it or might use it. In travel, this would usually be the holidaymaking public, or specific sections of the public depending on the type of holiday.

● **Marketing**

Everything within an organisation that's to do with selling the product or service, including the actual sales but also all the policymaking, research, advertising, and all sorts of other bits.

RESORT MANAGER

Resort managers (aka overseas managers) oversee a tour company's staff and operations in a resort and are responsible to the company for everything that goes on there.

It's a demanding and diverse role. You'll work as a rep and then a head rep for four or five years. By then, you'll really know the work and the area, and will have built good contacts. Your company promotes and trains you, and you are now in charge of creating good relations with suppliers (hoteliers, coach operators, etc.), developing and training staff (though not recruiting – that's done back home) and monitoring reps' performance – making sure they're where they should be. You'll also monitor client questionnaires to check that everything is hunky-dory. If it isn't, you'll address the relevant issues, perhaps by speaking with a hotel manager where the food isn't rated very highly, or with reps who haven't provided an adequate service.

Another aspect of the role is managing the finances. Each resort should cost a certain amount of money to run, and managers are there to create the best holiday for the guests while also balancing the levels of expenditure and income. 'This could be by offering an informal night out at a restaurant or an organised excursion,' says one resort manager. 'In Cyprus, we are able to offer quality excursions such as going to Israel and Egypt on a two- or three-day cruise. There are also the Roman sites and lots of other quality excursions to offer. There can be a lot of money coming in. Overseas managers are like mini managing directors of their own little company. In some resorts we're reaching in the region of half a million pounds' annual turnover. This is from excursions and other income generated in resort, such as local lets or local flights that we might organise. All this keeps the resort costs down, and then the brochure price can be more competitive. We also negotiate with suppliers. For instance, we might do car hire with a certain supplier so that we get a free car for the resort staff to operate, and organise welcome venues where we take guests to a restaurant or bar and the welcome drink is provided by the bar owner. Again, that's an expense that the company saves.'

WHAT'S IT LIKE?

'A lot of people are quite happy to be reps at forty or fifty,' says this manager. 'Others want a change. When I became resort manager I enjoyed it. I wasn't very good at it, though I didn't realise that until I got back to the UK. Trying to be strict with people is not my forte. Suddenly you're the boss of people you were working next to: it's very difficult to get over that hurdle.'

There seems to come a time for many reps when they suddenly can't take it any more: 'As soon as your patience goes, that's it,' our man says. Promotion meant he lost the hassle of daily contact with clients. 'But then you try to make yourself popular with the reps instead!'

He still had some contact with clients when he became manager, but only with the difficult ones: 'I only got to know very angry customers. But I like sorting out problems: it's always a challenge meeting someone who's very angry, and trying to turn the situation around. People could be abusive, and even physically violent. I

got people who the rep would phone me about in tears, unable to cope. But people change because they're with the manager. For them to see someone else tended to help the situation. It was a challenge, but it was nice to be able to support the reps.'

MOVING ON

There are great prospects for the right person. As this resort manager says: 'One regional manager for the western Mediterranean was only twenty-five when she got the post: she started out repping.'

Even if you don't become regional manager, there are still many possibilities in tour operations for people coming back to the UK after managing a resort. You might go into contracting, into product management, into training, or perhaps into the overseas department.

The overseas department is the UK back-up for the staff in resort. They ensure that people in resort have the staffing they require. They also look after training, uniform, image in resort, and organise and manage all the people. Working in the overseas department, you're involved on a daily basis with resorts and resort managers but you can liaise with the UK accounts area, customer relations, the sales area, and so on.

'You need to be experienced overseas to work here,' says one insider. 'If we had a member of staff who wasn't overseas experienced it would create problems. Overseas can only be run from knowing what people are going to do, and questioning those things. Very often there are brilliant

UK ideas that wouldn't work overseas. It's like with children, where Mum says: "I know what you're doing, even though I've got my back to you." You don't actually know what's happening because you're not there. That only comes from experience.'

In larger organisations some of the overseas functions may be performed by people in recruitment or training who have not worked overseas, but the core strategy and contact roles require that experience.

SKILLS YOU'LL NEED

You need strong overseas experience and ambition, together with a continuing desire for the overseas lifestyle and growing management ability. You'll gain some of this as head rep, which you might become after perhaps two or three years in resort.

PRACTICAL INSIDER INFORMATION ON HOW TO GET THE JOB

Not one you can go straight into. In your time repping, be nice to management, do your job well, and show management potential. Understand the commercial aspects; save money for the company, and lick your boss's toenails. It's bound to work.

SALES AND MARKETING

TRAVEL RATING: 2–8/10. Can be based abroad or travelling around, or you could be office-bound in the UK with only the usual business perks of reduced-rate travel.

MONEY: From about £14,000 as a trainee, perhaps less in the provinces. Managers earn from the mid-£20,000s upwards.

HOURS: Standard office hours plus more in times of crisis. Extra hours if you're travelling.

HEALTH RISK: 3–6/10. This is a normal commercial function, nothing too dangerous; how long you survive it depends on standard rat-race coping strategies.

PRESSURE RATING: 5/10. If sales drop it's your office they head to first. But not really more or less pressured than other office-based roles.

GLAMOUR RATING: 4/10. Marketing is on many people's list of preferred occupations – they think they'll drink lots of champagne and meet interesting people. Which they might, but it's more likely that they'll be doing routine back-room or sales work. 'It's perceived as glamorous,' says an insider. 'I'm not sure why.'

*Marketing means the sharp end: shifting the **product**. It covers all sorts of activities including sales of the product to the consumer (see sections on Travel Agent and Call Centre Staff for more on sales work) and formulating the policy you need before you can sell the product. That might mean commissioning market research, planning advertising, producing brochures, and all sorts of other activities. (See the Product Manager section for more on a pure marketing role.) This section is an overview of the sales and marketing function.*

There is sometimes a fine line between sales and marketing – what exactly do you call your role? An example is Vicki Good's job. She is called sales manager though much of what she does is actually marketing. Vicki works at the Hotel Garbe in Portugal. This is an 152-room hotel located on an Algarve beach, accommodating mostly holidaymakers. Her main responsibility is to ensure that the hotel has maximum occupancy at all times of the year. This involves **promotion**, **contracting** and **public relations**. She enjoys her work because every day is different. 'The best bits are dealing with people ... but then so are the worst bits,' she says.

She fell into the job by accident after working in hotels in the UK. 'At the interview for my first job in a hotel,' she says, 'I was told that people either love or hate the travel business – if you hate it you won't stay for more than six weeks; if you love it you will be in it for life. Twenty years later I can say this is true.' And after all this time she also says: 'There is very little "glamour" left for me.' But the work lives up to her expectations and she could now work in any resort hotel where the main business is holidaymakers.

Marketeers need to think ahead, probably a couple of years ahead with travel products that involve customers booking a holiday up to a year before they go. Other travel marketing may be shorter term, such as placing last-minute flight offers in the paper or shop window. Sales, as part of marketing, is more immediate. It also works ahead of itself in that strategy; planning and training all need to be in place before the sales are carried out, but the sales function itself is rarely as long drawn out as most marketing activities. So when a tour operator's 'holiday cycle' involves producing brochures for holidays up to two years ahead, while the **customer relations** work might be up to five years old, people like Martin Young, Panorama's Sales and Marketing Director, need to think long term. He deals with three areas of the company's operations: marketing (which includes public relations – PR), the sales side, and customer relations. 'My role is to think across all these areas and try to squeeze benefits out of them: how can sales and marketing together make five out of two plus two?

'The tour operator's product is intangible,' he explains. 'We're using someone else's hotel, transfer coaches, agents and retailers. You could ask: what part do we own and control? And the answer is: remarkably little. The phrase "the sharp end" is more true in other businesses, where branding and sales can have more of an effect. We're in the organisational business. Our success is down to each of the parts of the organisational chain working efficiently. In other industries you can have a crap product and a great image and get away with it, or a great product and no marketing, and it will still sell. But there's no point in me conjuring up fabulous sales if we don't deliver in resort. So marketing and selling are an important part of the process, but not as important as they are in other organisations.' He also explains that, whereas in some industries, such as cosmetics, rival companies all hate each other, 'in travel we all talk to each other, as we all buy off each other'.

Martin started off in non-travel sales and marketing. His first job involved sales work, so he understands the sales function from ground level. 'Marketing can be theoretical,' he says, 'using lots of **agencies** and creative, strategic thinking. Sales involves getting on with people and building relationships out of nothing.' Some marketeers have never themselves been in the sales function. 'Marketeers can demand the impossible from salespeople,' Martin says. 'They tend to look down their noses at salespeople, and vice versa: never the twain shall meet. But there are lots of issues common to both. It makes sense to spend time working in each of the sectors of the industry. They develop different sides of your personality, too.'

He spent this time selling and marketing **FMCG**. 'I was a brand manager, or a **product manager**:

those two terms are synonymous within FMCG. Then I saw the light, and realised that FMCG was extremely boring. The power and influence were moving from manufacturing to the retailing side, and the people doing all the interesting work were retailers.' He's talking here about supermarkets and other retailers packaging and marketing goods as their own, and leaving Martin and others, at the manufacturing end, with fewer marketing challenges. 'I was interested in travel, and qualified in marketing [he has a business studies degree], so I joined the small tour operator subsidiary of a charter airline as marketing manager.'

From there, he moved through a couple of other travel companies before landing at Panorama. 'People think of travel as the graveyard of any professional marketeer,' says Martin. 'These people are fooling themselves. I'm combining my business training with a subject I am passionate about.'

His career has developed strongly within travel: 'I've found that if people are enthusiastic and willing to learn and prove themselves in one area, then most companies are willing to give them a chance to develop.' He also points out that although many people move into travel from other areas, few leave. He's stayed put because it's fun: 'We are selling the one thing that people enjoy, that they want to buy. Try to get an interesting conversation going about other products that you might work with.' The annual holiday is most family's major regular purchase, and the one they don't mind spending their money on. 'People

spend forty-eight weeks of the year working, saving and thinking about the other four weeks, when they're on holiday. And as an industry it has grown, and looks set to continue growing. It's now the world's biggest employing industry.'

SKILLS YOU'LL NEED

'With the right personality, a willingness to work hard, and, early on, very long hours, it is possible to work and succeed in the travel industry,' says Vicki. And the main skills? 'Communication, communication, communication.'

Vicki has the equivalent of GCSEs, and Martin is a graduate: 'We don't specifically take graduates,' he says, 'though we do have some graduates in the call centre. We run our own informal training scheme.' Otherwise, he advises starting in retail (travel agency) as a good career move.

Going to university can take you in at a higher level: 'Good people are those with a reasonable grasp of the academics of marketing,' Martin continues, 'but prepared to marry that with the experience they can pick up. You need the basic principles you pick up at college, but also to understand how pragmatic experience can shape that. Also, you need to understand that business is about making profits.'

PRACTICAL INSIDER INFORMATION ON HOW TO GET THE JOB

Vicki recommends hotels, travel agents and tour operators as good ways in. 'With perseverance,' she says, 'there are a lot of openings.' Martin advises a direct approach: 'I identified a number of companies, and individuals within each company. These weren't the personnel departments (they are there to act on instructions) or marketing managers, but managing directors and chairmen. Start at the top and get it passed down to the relevant place. I'd already thought what I would do with a certain area, if I worked there. I wrote to them, and got a job, and then I did the same again.

'I can recommend it: pick who you want to work for; keep it short and snappy; tell them within the first sentence what you can do for them, and be prepared to justify that. It helps the company as they save on **recruitment fees**. My selling experience gave me the bottle to do it.'

He also describes how the managers within Panorama are on the lookout for good people: 'We suck people into the call centre, then you see the managers and directors circling like vultures. We've had people gone from the call centre to Operations, Commercial, Customer Relations and Marketing. This depends what stage in its development the business is at.

'Have the courage to write,' concludes Martin. 'The people who will stand out in people's minds are the people who make the effort to stand out in some way. You're always in with a shot.'

GLOSSARY

● **Agencies**

Independent companies in areas like advertising, market research, and so on. Most companies do not have the in-house resources to run all their own advertising, for instance, so they commission this from a specialist advertising agency.

● **Contracting**

Arranging the contracts to rent the hotel's rooms. (See the Contractor section for details of this.)

● **Customer relations**

Sorting out customer queries and complaints, etc. after departure, as opposed to customer services, which occurs pre-departure. These may include long-term disputes between the customer and the tour operator, in some cases involving other parties, which can take years to resolve.

● **FMCG**

Fast Moving Consumer Goods. These are exactly what you'd expect from the term: standard consumer items that leave the shelves quickly. Martin's FMCC experience was with a large drinks company.

● **Networking**

Using your contacts and new people you meet to build up a 'web' of useful contacts, who are mutually helpful when you need things in your work.

● **Product**

The thing you're selling. In this case, it's a package holiday.

● **Product manager**

See the separate section on this role.

● **Promotion**

Promoting the product. This can be through word of mouth and **networking**, handing out leaflets at trade fairs, advertising, and so on.

● **Public relations**

When a company or other organisation communicates less formally than it does through advertising or other promotions. This

might mean talking to journalists in
the hope that they will write an
article about your hotel, sending out
press releases about special events,
holding special weekends and inviting
people you want to communicate
with, and so on.

● **Recruitment fees**

When companies need people, they
may go to recruitment agencies.
These agencies offer a free service to
individual job-hunters but charge
organisations: it could cost them 10 or
15 per cent of the annual salary,
which translates into a lot of money.
If companies can get good people
without using an agency, they'll go
that route.

TOUR MANAGER

The UK is the starting point for many visitors to Europe, and of these a fair few want to get on a coach and do the whirlwind tour. These tours usually start with some time spent travelling in the UK and then continue on to the Continent (though some are totally UK-based). The travellers need looking after... and that's where you come in.

Tour managers – also known as tour directors – accompany groups of tourists travelling by coach in the UK and abroad. They are responsible for all communications: tour guiding, hotel checking-in, medical emergencies, and possibly even noise control if you get a rowdy group to manage. 'The nature of each tour is fundamentally different,' says one insider, 'though the minutiae of the tours are the same: staying in the same hotels, touring the same regions. We're looking at how the outside [i.e. the country and culture visited] is integrated into the minds of the people on the inside.'

A more down-to-earth view comes from Angie, who worked several summers as a tour manager while she was a student. 'The money was brilliant: £1,000 a week, mostly tips. But it was hard work. You're supposed to research all the information you need but you can't know everything. One trip included a visit to Stirling Castle and I'd never been there before. I got everyone off the coach – they were all middle-aged Americans, and they didn't always want to get off and sightsee – and stood them in front of Stirling Castle and started my talk about it and its history and said that although it might seem smaller than they'd expected, it was a very important place, and all that. Then the driver came and nudged me and said: "Look over there." Behind us was Stirling Castle. I'd been showing them completely the wrong place.'

One large sector of the market is American teenagers coming to the UK as the starting point for the European culture tour. You'll be recruited to look after the group for the duration, and although you need to be able to give basic information about the sights, you are there primarily to ensure that all the arrangements run smoothly and to deal with any problems. These can include sorting out accommodation that has been double-booked or being woken by the hotel manager in the middle of the night with noise complaints. The coach could break down; you might have a medical emergency. Although there is a driver, you are in charge.

The typical day includes getting the group going, driving to a new destination and handing over to a locally qualified guide. You pay the group's entrance charges to the attraction and come along on the tour. Later, you might take the group to a factory or craft centre to watch goods being made: leather in Italy, perfume in Paris. The commission on anything they buy at the end of visits such as these is a part of your pay, and can be substantial. The day may entail further visits, and you may be expected to socialise in the evening.

As well as the commission element of your pay, some nationalities tip well. You might earn £500 in tips alone after a week taking Americans on tour, for instance, though be warned that some other nationalities hardly tip at all.

Some tour managers work trips back to back on six-month contracts and earn plenty this way, then perhaps take the winter off to do something else, but it's exhausting work, and many people would say that they need some sort of rest between trips, and certainly after an extended period. 'Most people burn out,' says Linda, who spends some of her time as a tour manager. 'It's very tiring. I couldn't do it back to back like that: it's too stressful.' It's also, she says, 'a job of extremes. You can have a lovely day then the next day can all go horribly wrong.'

TRAINING

A tour company will give you an initial two- or three-day training course on the use of the microphone, what to say in any particular situation, how to deal with emergencies, and so on. You are expected to do your own research on all tour stops, though not in great depth, as local guides will come on board to tell your group about some of the places you visit.

'This work creates its own dynamic: there's only a certain amount of training you can do,' says Paul Mattesini, who recruits for a large tour company. 'You discover, from your experience of it, whether it's for you. As with teaching, you can do all the learning, but eventually you have to go out and interact.'

SKILLS YOU'LL NEED

● Fluency in English and at least one additional language, though a few tour managers who work within the UK speak only English.
● Travel experience in Europe and some city knowledge. You need to know the sights, their history, culture and current developments. On your application you will be specifically

asked which cities and areas of the UK and Europe you know, and how well. Also, any experience of the tourist industry is useful. For educational tours, experience as a teacher or language teacher will help.

● Organisational skills. You need to be able to handle the background logistics of a tour so that when you are with the group you don't have to worry about this aspect and are free to help them make the most of their time.

● Flexibility. There is a set framework and when problems arise you need to deal with them effectively within this framework.

● A service attitude. You are there to provide the best holiday or educational tour for your customers. As with most jobs in the travel business, this professional attitude is essential.

● Independence. Many tour companies are looking for (among others) young graduates who have travelled and lived away from home.

● Age 23-plus, though occasionally tour managers are younger. Some are in their sixties.

● You don't need any specific qualifications, but the better-established operators prefer to take experienced tour managers.

PRACTICAL INSIDER INFORMATION ON HOW TO GET THE JOB

'We advertise in the national press and in selected magazines that go into the universities,' says Paul Mattesini. 'Our offices around Europe do the same thing. This year we had a thousand applications across Europe.' Applicants are sent information about the work, and an application form. 'People do well to get to our selection day,' Paul says. His company runs a day's group interview, and then successful applicants are invited to a residential training weekend. 'We run through the logistics of the job, do role plays, get on a coach. This is part of the selection and training process.' People aren't paid to attend this weekend, though their expenses are paid once they have completed their first tour for the company.

Other companies have different recruitment procedures, though the selectors are looking for the same things. 'After the basic criteria,' says Paul, 'I'm using my own judgement. There are so many grey areas that it's difficult to specify the criteria we look for. If I look at four of our best tour directors and ask what they have in common, I'd say nothing, above the basics that are needed for the work.

'I did it full-time for seven years. I didn't think, initially, I had the personality for the work, but you develop your own tour persona.'

All tour managers are employed on a freelance, seasonal basis, and newly trained tour managers could probably expect to work only around Easter and in the summer. There is no guarantee of work.

USEFUL ADDRESSES

Contact your tourist board for the names of tour companies (see the listing in Appendix 1).

TOURIST INFORMATION OFFICER

TRAVEL RATING: 2–6/10. Low if you're based in the UK, with local travel in low season and possibly some foreign travel, but you could live and work abroad.

MONEY: Starts at about £8,000 for UK beginners.

HOURS: Office hours plus weekends, but in high season you may be called on to do overtime when the office stays open into the evenings.

HEALTH RISK: 1/10. Stabbing by a mad tourist is the main risk but is, as yet, unreported in the UK press.

PRESSURE RATING: 5/10. It'll be quiet and even a little tedious, and then a coachload of foreigners appear and shout together in a language you don't understand.

GLAMOUR RATING: 2/10. Someone famous may, one day, wander into the office. But if they're very famous, they'll get someone else to wander in for them.

All major towns and cities have Tourist Information Centres (TICs) where visitors can go to pick up a map, book a hotel or ask anything about the place and its environs. The people who work here have all this information at their fingertips. They need to find the required information and deal with a diverse public, some of whom speak no English.

If you're happy dealing with travelling visitors rather than travelling yourself, this can be a great job. It's a good mix of administration, working with the public and using languages.

Karen works in a TIC in a city on the 'tourist trail'. 'We get a lot of Americans and Japanese,' she says. 'Day-trippers are shown around by their guide but those staying longer often want to go off on their own, and this is their first port of call.' There is also a good mix of European visitors. The staff in her office speak a total of nine languages between them, including Japanese. 'The Eastern languages are becoming more important,' she says. 'It's difficult to get people who are fluent. People who learn Japanese and similar languages often go to work in business, not tourism.'

Karen is employed by her local authority, which has sponsored three of the staff to learn a second foreign language so that the overall range they offer is broader. 'Most of us speak French and German, and some of us Spanish. It's the less common languages that are in demand.'

Staff take turns to sit at the front desk, perhaps alone on quiet days in a smaller office, or as one of a team. Typical queries from visitors include where to find a good hotel or restaurant, how to get to the airport, how to find medical or dental services. People may ask questions about other parts of the country and for advice on travelling around. You'll make hotel reservations, book tickets for coach tours and reserve theatre tickets. This entails using different research methods, including guidebooks, brochures and timetables, though more and more the research is done on the Internet.

You'll get asked all sorts of questions, including silly ones. 'People leave their brains behind when they go on holiday,' says Karen. 'You can tell that these are intelligent, competent and even charming people in real life, but some of them morph into customers from hell. They come in, barge to the front of the queue, ignore the fact that you are on the telephone researching something for the customer you are dealing with, and demand to know why their hotel is so poor. You need a lot of tact and patience and sometimes to be very firm. We work in a team, though, so there should always be somebody free to come through from the back and help you with particularly difficult customers. Most people are polite. They realise that we are representing the city, not running it. And it's lovely when customers thank you for all the work you do, and even come back in with cards or chocolates: it can be very rewarding.'

When you're not at the front desk you'll be collating information behind the scenes, updating that already on file, and answering telephone and postal queries. 'We get a lot of post,' says Karen. 'Often we reply with standard literature but sometimes we need to write a formal letter to an enquirer. You need a reasonable level of the written language.'

There are travel opportunities. You might be asked to travel abroad to help represent your town at a European or international marketing fair. Here you'd work on a stand at a huge convention, promoting your city's tourism opportunities to tour operators and others who might want to take a group to the UK. This job is more likely to fall to a local government marketing officer, though – it depends on your employer. Also, in low season when there's less work in the office, you will go on day trips to local places of interest so that you can promote them more knowledgeably to your customers.

There are opportunities for management posts within the TIC. These involve setting up systems, running the office, buying in books, maps and postcards for sale, liaising with other tourism departments and organisations, training staff, and so on. Some people go on from TICs into marketing and other tourism work, or may find similar work abroad in European TICs if their languages are good enough.

SKILLS YOU'LL NEED

You need fluency in at least one additional language, though qualifications aren't necessary. You also need a reasonable level of the written language. You might also be expected to learn a third or further language to provide a broader coverage for visitors. You need to enjoy talking to new people, sometimes under pressure, as the office can get very busy at peak times. Customers might be distressed or worried and need a calm, problem-solving approach.

There are no standard qualifications necessary but an employer will probably ask for a minimum of five good GCSEs. Many people have degrees or vocational qualifications such as a GNVQ in Leisure and Tourism.

You'll need to be organised and happy using the telephone and computer. Basic business skills such as letter-writing are also useful. You'll be dealing with money and may need to take responsibility for this, cashing up and banking at the end of the day, so you need to be numerate.

PRACTICAL INSIDER INFORMATION ON HOW TO GET THE JOB

Watch the local press for job vacancies. There's usually a low staff turnover, though: if you're keen, try going in and requesting to speak to the manager. Ask to spend some time helping out voluntarily and to be considered when a post arises.

There are also regional and national tourist offices and boards: try writing for recruitment information.

TRAINING MANAGER

Training managers and staff work to improve the skills of the people within their organisation. Other trainers work freelance and dive into needy workplaces to train the staff there.

All large organisations have a training department – though this could consist of somebody buying in training from other agencies rather than running training sessions themselves. There's far more emphasis on training within the travel industry than there used to be, although it's always been fairly good. But where sometimes reps might have flown out to resort and done their own thing, and travel agents could bumble along picking it up as they went, it's now more regulated and professional.

As a beginner to repping you're likely to be given an induction course lasting several weeks, followed by regular top-ups. In agencies, you could study for the travel NVQs and various other qualifications such as a ticketing certificate. In all areas there will be specific training tailored to your work development needs. This book doesn't go into detail about training, as employers will tell you what their training schemes involve. Appendix 3 gives a basic introduction. This section is about what it's like to train people, but you may find it useful to read it anyway, as you'll see the plans travel companies may have for you.

TRAINING WITHIN TRAVEL

Before you start work you'll do lots of academic and/or vocational study. Then, when you get a job, you might become part of a formal training scheme. Within your organisation there will be a human resources department working alongside a training department, pulling all these elements together to ensure that you are properly trained for what you do, and maybe devising specially tailored courses for your particular needs.

Andrew Farr is training manager with the Panorama Holiday Group. His job is to train overseas people: at the moment he is devising training courses for reps in sales skills (to help them sell excursions to customers) and in customer care. He will take these courses overseas for a six-week block to the various resorts where a training need has been identified. 'They'll get one day's training on this. I'm happy doing what I'm doing because I can use my ideas of how to get the best out of people, and write training modules. I can train reps to be excellent reps.' It wasn't part of his great career plan. He spent two years as a rep then seven years in the theatre before going back to repping and overseas management: 'It's not anything I'd have thought I would do, though I did think of teaching. It was recognised that as a Jack-of-all-trades who can entertain, I could do this. But I've no formal training in training.' Andrew is qualified by experience: 'I think I was an excellent rep and I want those standards to continue. I'm really happy doing that.'

There are so many differences between working in the UK and working in resort that you couldn't train reps unless you had plenty of experience working as one, and probably managing them, too. Here the route is clearly to start in repping. Hoda Lacey runs a travel training consultancy called It's All About People. As well as repping she has worked for a tour operator and as a customer relations manager. She works with people skills, not the technical side. 'I teach how to give better service, communication skills, management strategy, empathy skills, tele-selling skills, and so on,' she explains. 'I work as an associate for other training companies, for tour operators, retail travel agents and suppliers. A typical thing might be a travel agent saying that staff communications skills are not very good.' She will then look at the whole structure of that part of the business and plan her training accordingly.

MANAGERS CARRYING OUT TRAINING

As well as training given by the training department, individual managers also train their staff informally on-the-job and sometimes in formal sessions. They are experts in their roles and have risen through the ranks by doing the work themselves, so they know what they're talking about. That in itself doesn't mean that they necessarily make good trainers. 'When you run a training session and use resources like an overhead projector, people don't necessarily remember it,' says Andrew Farr. 'If you do things with humour people are more inclined to remember it.' There are many ways of effectively communicating information and skills so that they will be remembered and used in the workplace, and managers such as Andrew have their own, often individual, approaches to their work. And there is always a need for training in the workplace: 'It makes my blood boil when I see reps where customer service is so let down. People need to be told,' he believes.

SKILLS YOU'LL NEED

Good training managers have a natural empathy with people. They also have knowledge and skills gained through their own work experience. They need a good sense of humour, and to enjoy standing up in front of others and performing as well as working one to one. Organisational and technical skills are also important for putting together and delivering a training session that may involve computer technology.

PRACTICAL INSIDER INFORMATION ON HOW TO GET THE JOB

'Start as a rep,' says Andrew Farr. 'I'm very pleased with what I'm doing but in the past I could never envisage the type of job I could ever have. I've never had a career plan at all. There are opportunities for a career in travel and the best place to start is overseas.' Training is often something people move into after gaining experience and coming to enjoy the staff development and training side of management.

TRAINS

TRAVEL RATING: 6/10, although you could be office-bound, depending on your role. Most travel is UK-based and concentrates on one or a number of routes. You might venture through the Channel Tunnel.

MONEY: From about £8,000 in customer services roles, £13,000 as a trainee driver; management and head office jobs follow salaries in other industries.

HOURS: On the trains, up to 11-hour shifts, any time over 24 hours and weekends. Maybe working a roster with four weeks on and one off.

HEALTH RISK: 3/10. The strict rules against drinking even a teeny bit before your shift will cut your hangovers, but shift work might do you in instead.

PRESSURE RATING: 7/10. Driving trains is a responsible business and requires constant concentration over long periods. Other roles involving customer service are also demanding and pressured.

GLAMOUR RATING: With the press our railways get minus ten out of ten. But this should change once new investment takes effect.

Our railways have been through a time of huge change, from the days when they were a nationalised industry receiving less and less investment to the recent sell-off to private companies which operate trains in different regions and have injected new money into the system. They are still investing in new stock and new staff and once the changes are in place the railways should receive a better press (they hope). In the meantime, it's a good time to join, in anticipation of a new golden era of the railways.

There are many different train operating companies in the UK. (These are separate from the company that maintains the track and infrastructure.) They are closely regulated, both from a safety point of view and to ensure that their service is adequate: trains are our only transport service required to meet punctuality targets, for instance.

The operating companies recruit for a wide range of jobs and careers, some working directly with the public and others in driving, technical and management roles. These include working on the trains: each train has one driver, one train manager, a senior steward, and perhaps other stewards and catering staff. People are needed for work in stations, and on the engineering side of the business – research this through your engineering course and specialist careers adviser.

DRIVER

It's solitary work as you are on your own in the cab, though at your destination there's a mess room where you'll mix with other drivers. It's also shift work and it can be long hours: a standard week is 37 hours, but you might work 45 hours one week then less the next, with shifts of up to 11 hours. Your work will be spread across the entire week, including weekends and nights. 'We have a very strict drink and drugs policy,' says Amanda Price of Virgin Trains, 'with random screening. This means that if you go out with your mates on a Saturday night and you are working on Sunday morning, you won't be able to drink. This can be a problem for the younger generation, but having a whole week off between rosters is a great benefit.'

New drivers with Virgin Trains start on £13,500. They receive twelve months' training, and if they complete this successfully their salary rises to £24,300 plus allowances. You're not classed as an experienced driver until you've worked for a number of years more, probably about three, when your pay rises to £27,000 plus allowances. These allowances are an additional £3,000 for working 26 Sundays in the year, and another £3,000 for a good attendance record (with low sickness levels, etc.). There is an additional bonus for working some of your rest days, but there are regulations that only allow you to work thirteen days in a row.

'There's also a big emphasis on getting women drivers,' says Amanda. 'They are under-represented in train driving, and we are looking for more.'

TRAIN MANAGER

This is the job formerly known as 'guard'. You'll go along the train dealing with customer service queries, checking tickets and so on. You can earn £22,000 on prime routes, perhaps £18,000 on others. You'll probably start as a steward then progress to senior steward. If you want promotion to train manager you'll go into a pool, wait for a vacancy then apply.

SERVICE MANAGER

You'll look after all the catering and customer services on a train. On services with a number of first-class coaches there could be seven or eight catering staff: one person working the buffet car for standard-class passengers, and then people manning the juice trolley and serving tea, coffee, toast and silver-service breakfasts, say, to first-class passengers.

STATION STAFF

You might work as a booking clerk, issuing tickets and other products, as well as providing customer information. You need to be numerate and have good customer service skills. As a station assistant you'll be responsible for the safe dispatch of trains, customer care, and keeping the station in good order. Station managers are responsible for the whole station or a number of stations, including reaching sales targets. You'll monitor your staff, train them, oversee ticketing, rostering, budgets, health and safety, and so on.

MANAGER

Because the operating companies are relatively new, some are still putting their management recruitment and training policies into place. Some operate graduate training schemes for managers while others develop their management staff mainly from people already working there, so promotion opportunities can be excellent. Amanda Price is a good example: she is now People Development Manager for Virgin Trains, but started on a government training scheme similar to National Traineeships. 'We went into different areas within the railways,' she says, 'and visited stations and depots. After about three months I was offered a job by British Rail in their data input centre, inputting time sheets and family railcards, and so on. I really enjoyed it: it was fun, and nice to be earning a wage at that age. It was valuable in the fact that I learned about the railways and what it's all about.' She stayed for two years and then, because BR had an internal vacancy list covering the whole of the company, was able to move sideways into other roles. 'I spent two years in a reprographic studio, which I didn't especially like, then got a job in personnel.' Within six months she was heading up that section, and then a year later she moved across to manage external recruitment for her region.

After restructuring, she worked in a training centre for three years. Then she got her first management post, as a welfare and equal opportunities manager. 'I did a lot of background research before that interview,' she remembers.

Then Virgin took over the region and, after a while, she became recruitment manager for Virgin Trains. 'British Rail, and now Virgin, are very good at giving opportunities for training. They believe in developing their own people, if you want to do day release, for instance. I did a certificate and they paid for that. Now they are going to support me through a degree. If you come out of school with GCSEs they will support you, as they have me for the last fifteen years.' Although Virgin don't currently have a graduate training scheme, they are looking to introduce one soon.

SKILLS YOU'LL NEED

All work in the railway companies is customer-orientated so you'll need the same customer care skills as for travel generally, and probably some experience, such as working in a shop or other role. Specific jobs carry their own requirements, and you may find work without formal academic qualifications. Most of these jobs require some shift work.

You need to be 21 or over to train as a driver. You don't need any specific previous experience or a driving licence, though you have to be able to get to work at times when public transport is not running. Recruiters like people who have already worked shifts, as they are more likely to stay in the job, but this is not essential. You need to be a team player in case things go wrong, but you also have to be happy with your own company. You must also be in good health in order to pass a medical assessment (covering hearing, eyesight and colour vision, and more).

Recruiters are not looking for specific skills in their driver applicants but for the right attitude. 'We are looking for people who are customer-focused,' says Amanda Price, 'and who have an understanding of the importance of safety. They need good communication skills and to enjoy working with people. And it's great if they have some mechanical understanding.' You also need to be able to follow rules and procedures, be able to concentrate for long periods of time, and be flexible in order to work the antisocial hours.

PRACTICAL INSIDER INFORMATION ON HOW TO GET THE JOB

Train companies advertise in local papers and on their websites when they're looking for people for a whole range of jobs, including those mentioned above, where you don't need prior experience in the railway industry. They also attend the larger job and recruitment fairs, where you could find out more about the spread of jobs and perhaps have a first informal interview.

Many people are interested in driving work, and if that's the case with you it's a good time to apply. With the industry working towards more frequent services and with more new trains, there is currently a shortage, which will probably last over the next five years until new investment and services have levelled out. 'Phone the train operating companies,' says Amanda Price, 'or write in with your CV and get yourself logged on to their system. Ask about vacancies. They should contact you in the future even if there are no vacancies at that time.' Applicants who are invited for interview start with tests such as a rules ability test, to see if you can

follow rules, and a personality questionnaire based on safety issues. There are no 'right' answers to this sort of test; rather you state how you would cope with certain situations. This test reveals areas to be explored further by recruiters at interview. There are also concentration tests.

If you're successful at first interview, you'll go on to the next stage, a train crew assessment. This includes a reaction test, a concentration test and a trainability test (to see if you will be able to absorb twelve months of training). Then there's a criteria-based interview, which means that you talk about your real-life experiences. For instance, you might be asked to describe your achievements, or an emergency situation you've experienced. The interviewers note what you have done in the past, and judge how likely you are to react correctly to situations in the future.

You can also opt to pay for the train crew assessment test yourself. It costs about £150, and if you pass it's valid for two years. 'Any train operating companies will probably be interested to see you if you've passed,' says Amanda. 'When it's taken in that situation, probably about forty per cent of people pass. It requires a lot of concentration: you'll come out exhausted.' Amanda recommends that you play console and computer games to prepare for the assessment. 'The fighting games are reaction games,' she says. 'They improve your reactions to sight and sound.' Contact the operating companies for information on taking the test.

Another way to train as a driver is to come into a railway company at a different level. That way you can gain a knowledge of trains and the industry, and after a couple of years apply for a trainee driver's job.

TRANSFER REPRESENTATIVE

Transfer reps are the 'meeters and greeters' who collect holidaymakers from the airport, deliver them to their accommodation and collect them again at the end of their holiday. Many of these jobs are based in resort, but you can also do this work on coach-based trips from the UK, in which case you'll probably be known as a travel courier (see below).

If you work for a small tour operator, or in a resort with only a few flights each week, then you might combine this work with other general holiday repping duties. But in the larger resorts, especially where there are flights arriving and departing every day, then you'd be employed as a specialist transfer rep.

THE WORK

As a transfer rep you're responsible for finding incoming passengers, greeting and reassuring them, helping them with any problems, getting them on the right coach with the right luggage, and delivering them to the right accommodation. From there, they are somebody else's responsibility until you collect them at the end of their holiday.

Hiccups in this well-thought-out plan might include being unable to find the passengers (if your list is wrong, perhaps), or having too many arrive (for the same reason). They might have lost their luggage or experience difficulties with their passports or currency. You need to be able to deal with anything like this efficiently while reassuring the passengers that all's well.

Once on the coach, you tell your passengers a little about the area, and the procedure once they get to their accommodation.

WHAT'S IT LIKE?

'It's the best of the best,' says Andrew Farr, Panorama's training manager. 'You get all the best bits and none of the bad bits. You're there at the start of their holidays, when you can give a good impression. When they get off the coach, you've done your job. If they find that the rooms are all full, you're not the one to tackle all that. The complaints period is the first twenty-four to thirty-six hours. Two weeks later, generally, people are fine. When you pick them up, people have had a good holiday and you get all the credit. All the glory, none of the pain.'

It can be a long job, especially when there are aircraft delays. 'I don't mind the hours,' says Andrew. 'You could have a six- or seven-hour flight delay, and you stay with your passengers and get lots of flak. But it's the most enjoyable job in the whole of repping. I like being on that microphone in front of all those people, showing off; and I like trying to make people laugh. First and last impressions are so important.'

CAREER PROGRESSION

Repping is generally a short-term job, but many experienced reps later go into transfer repping as a part-time alternative. In smaller resorts there may not be enough flights or guests to justify a full-time transfer rep, so some part-timers live locally and do this as one of their professional activities, or as a retirement job. Heather works this way. She lives on the Algarve coast of Portugal and does transfers to and from Faro airport when she's needed. 'I only fill in when they are desperate,' she says. 'I used to be a rep here and they know me.' On the return transfer, she picks up passengers at five to ten hotels in resort. The guests are usually

there and ready, but not always: 'On a recent bus we had one couple who hadn't packed and weren't ready at all, and another that had already left in a taxi. We waited for the first ones, and hoped that the others got there under their own steam: they probably wanted to see something on the way there, do some last-minute sightseeing.'

Heather ensures they are in the right check-in queue. 'I hang around for as long as I can, but new guests come through from the same aircraft so I can't stay until they're all checked in. Most people are sensible enough to get themselves on the aeroplane.'

She describes the long hours: 'Last weekend I started at three on Friday afternoon and didn't get to bed properly until four on Monday morning. I was home at times but it's pretty non-stop.'

'Generally, it's not a job on which you can survive,' says Andrew Farr about the money, 'unless you're in the larger resorts with flights every day, when you'd be salaried.'

You may progress to become airport controller. This entails organising the transfers, making sure the reps are there to greet people, dealing with people who have lost luggage, seeing that all the coaches have got proper display signs, and so on.

TRAVEL COURIER

Travel couriers are a combination of a transfer rep and a tour manager (see separate section). They join a coach party in the UK at the beginning of a trip and perform the same greeting and administrative duties as tour managers and transfer reps. During the trip they commentate on places of interest and ensure that things run smoothly at overnight stopovers. When they reach their destination they leave their passengers and collect another set for the journey home. Most couriers are freelance and work on fixed-term contracts, often only in the high-season months.

SKILLS YOU'LL NEED

You need the same people skills as for a repping job, with special emphasis on administrative skills ... you mustn't lose a passenger! (See the sections on Holiday Representative and Tour Manager for an overview of these skills.) Additionally, you need to be able to organise people tactfully, as the logistics of the whole trip depend on their co-operation.

You need to be fluent in the language of the country where you are working. This is more important than for general holiday reps as you may need to sort out complex immigration or logistical problems. As Andrew puts it: 'A language is very beneficial so that you can sort out things with people at airports and with the drivers. You never want to make an enemy of your driver, ever. You'll not get bags put on for you or taken off for you, no favours, no diversions to extra hotels, etc.'

PRACTICAL INSIDER INFORMATION ON HOW TO GET THE JOB

The same applies here as for general holiday repping if you want to work in resort. Employers like to see evidence of a language and experience of living abroad.

For travel courier work, you need to apply for jobs advertised in the trade or national press, or write on spec to the tour operators. You should apply in the autumn for the next summer season. There is also work in ski resorts, and you should apply the preceding summer for these jobs.

TRAVEL AGENT

TRAVEL RATING: 3/10. You're office-based but tour operators hand out **educationals** to get you abroad. And there's subsidised travel and, of course, access to the best deals going.

MONEY: You could start on £8,000 rising to £10,000 after a few years. A shop manager might earn £16,000 or more. There's also commission, which can be substantial if you're good, and with the right employer.

HOURS: Generally shop hours including weekends, sometimes on a rolling rota system. Longer hours are becoming commonplace.

HEALTH RISK: 2/10. Holidaymakers are generally happy and therefore likely to be nice to you. You won't be able to afford too much high living, so your liver will remain healthy.

PRESSURE RATING: 6/10. Surprisingly tough, in fact, despite the laid-back image. Change in the business is bringing tighter margins, so the pressure is on for you to keep selling.

GLAMOUR RATING: 3/10. 'A lot of young people have incorrectly thought-out ideas of how glamorous it is. I would not say it's a glamorous job at all; it's a very hard graft job.'

This is the sharp end of travel: selling to the public. Typically, travel agents have a high-street shop where customers can browse then buy travel products. Staff, or 'consultants', working within travel agencies advise their clients on the best product for their needs, check availability, get the best deal, and book it. The agent then takes a commission from the supplier. For instance, when booking a flight, traditionally the travel agent would receive 10 per cent of the cost of the flight, and the airline would get the other 90 per cent.

It's a sales job, but it's not like selling something like car insurance: people *want* to go on holiday. Rosalind Wolfarth is an independent travel agent who owns her agency, Anders Travel. This is not part of one of the big chains of travel agencies, so she can run it as she pleases. She describes the work like this: 'The customer comes in and they say what they want and I will try and go out to buy to their specifications. That principle is the same for a tailor-made holiday or for flights only.'

As a travel agent you advise clients about resorts and travel arrangements, sell brochure holidays, tickets for transport such as flights, car hire and possibly coach and rail, accommodation, travel insurance, organise passport and visa collection, and possibly book theatre and events tickets.

You need a broad knowledge of the destinations the customer is interested in, the types of package that might suit them, and how to research the products on offer. 'Everybody has their favourite ways of procuring information,' says Rosalind, 'some of which is available to anybody on screens. But you can opt to get what are effectively journals on disk, such as databases for air fares or late availability, which are updated on a regular basis. Those are very useful, and they are what we tend to use.' Many agencies are fully automated, with computer reservation systems linked to tour operator and airline databases, though you'll also make bookings by telephone.

When she's looking through a brochure with a client, Rosalind is reading between the lines, as if she were booking her own holiday, and this is where her experience is important. 'One of the problems with the industry is that you get a lot of eighteen-year-olds who don't know what they're talking about,' she says, although there are of course many skilled young travel consultants too. 'I look at several brochures. We make extensive use of things like gazetteers to get a less biased opinion.

'We're talking about a huge world out there. I would say to do this job effectively, you have to have your brain switched on the whole time. It isn't easy to find everything. There are easy ways to get into packages but if you're looking for something non-packaged it can be quite complex to set it up. That's by far the nicest part of it: doing the different things is far more interesting.'

The sales element is an important part of the work, and you'll be trained to help you do this. Jane Barter is a Holiday Hypermarket manager, and explains: 'In the high-street agencies, and here, we have **closing-the-sale** training, establishing customers' needs, customer service, asking the right questions: everything to do with closing the sale. In sales, the customer buys "you" before they buy the product. If we've given a really good service and built up a really good rapport with them, nine times out of ten, even if they don't book it there and then, they will come back. We will try to overcome their objections, such as: "I can't book today, I need to phone my other half." We say: "Would you like to use the phone?" Or: "I really don't want to spend that much money." We say: "This is exactly the hotel you want; it's got the children's club." We try to sell them the benefits of what they wanted. But if they don't book, we find that they will come back. People do want a good service.' Rosalind Wolfarth agrees: 'Effectively we are salespeople, but we try and think of ourselves as purchasers for our clients. That's my philosophy.'

Good travel agents rely on repeat business, and some agencies have customers coming back to them every time they go on holiday. Often a customer will come back after the holiday and tell you what it was like, how much they enjoyed it, and thank you for your part in that.

OTHER ASPECTS OF THE JOB

Travel agents have other tasks apart from this customer service role. Sales create administration, so you will need to fill in forms, call the customer to check details, receive tickets near the date of travel, dispatch tickets, check details on invoices, type letters, send out confirmations, and so on. You generally fit this admin around serving your customers. Some agencies employ separate admin people to do most or all of this work, perhaps one admin for four or five sales staff, but this is not always economical, and anyway, there are always odds and ends of admin to do. (See Administrator section.)

Another part of the role is answering telephone queries. Sometimes these are from customers who have already visited and want an update, or perhaps have changed their requirements. Other calls might come from new customers with questions who may come in later to book, or book over the phone by credit card. Some agencies have specialist sections for this; others are entirely devoted to selling by telephone.

You might also fill the brochures racks and keep them tidy. Brochures arrive in large numbers and are stored at the back of most shops, but it's important that, before they go on the shelves, they are stamped with the agency name and contact details so that customers who take them away know where to go to book their holiday.

Travel consultants also help customers sort out any problems with the holidays or services they have booked. A customer might have a complaint that was not dealt with in resort, for one reason or another, and ask you to help them deal with it. Jane Barter says: 'I think people expect so much now. They know a lot more of

what they are entitled to. You do your best and find them the holiday they want. If they've got a problem with their holiday after they've come back, and they want us to write a letter to the tour company for them, then we will look after their complaint.'

Some travel agencies also deal in foreign exchange. You might do this alongside your other roles if you are trained to, or there might be other people in the agency who do only this. (See the Foreign Exchange section.)

WHAT IT'S LIKE WORKING IN AN AGENCY

'A high-street travel agency is basically an office and there's no atmosphere,' says Hayley Williams. But just because it feels like an office doesn't mean the work is dull. Clarissa Bowley also spent time in a high-street travel agency: 'It was a lot busier than I thought it was going to be. There was a lot of admin and phone work, and foreign exchange as well. It was good but it was hard work. We had to do overtime, sometimes serving someone after we shut, and then we'd have to do the admin after that. It was a lot busier on Saturdays and Sundays. Also, the phone was always ringing and you had to phone people back. Sometimes you want to concentrate on who you're serving at the time, so it can be off-putting for the customer, though you get used to it after a time. I know some people who have done agency work and have found it too hard.'

'I can honestly say that the one thing I am not is bored in this business,' says Rosalind. 'I get frustrated; I get furious at times, but I never get bored. Because the personalities are different I think it's actually rather nice. If you're prepared to put up with the fact that you aren't necessarily treated especially well by a lot of people it's OK, because there are people who do treat you properly and who are appreciative of what you do.'

'I didn't get bored unless it was really quiet,' agrees Clarissa. 'There are so many things you can get on with, like looking out the brochures or invoices, doing the window cards. And when you book it, it does make you feel good that they've got what they want, and of course you get the commission as well.'

It's very much a team role, too: 'We ask one another: "What was the research you did last week?"' says Rosalind. 'So you know you've got other people out there who can help you with your work. Everybody in travel should tell you that nobody in **retail** knows everything. If you don't know that you don't know everything, you've got a big problem.'

And as in any job, there are times when you wish you were anywhere else. 'Sometimes it really is teeth-gritting,' says Rosalind. 'A colleague was here until six-fifteen yesterday with a client who was here from half past four. Eventually she got a booking but even when he'd decided what he wanted to do he still wanted us to check several other things just in case there was something else that might crop up. But a lot of people have gone out of it and come back into it: I've actually employed people several times over. They don't mind doing it again: you very rarely get that in

anything.' And as Clarissa says: 'Travel isn't a really well-paid industry, but if you enjoy selling holidays to different places and meeting lots of different people then I'd say go for it.'

HOW IT ALL WORKS

Travel agencies make their money on commissions from the products they sell. It's always been this way, with set commission rates from the airlines, tour operators and others. This encourages you to sell as much as you can to the customer. For instance, if someone booked a business-class air ticket rather than an economy ticket, this would earn more for the agency, and, depending on the commission scheme, more for you too. Yet, as Rosalind says: 'We won't sell something that we actually don't think is going to suit the client.'

Although they would deny it, this is not always the case with the chains of travel agencies, most of which are owned by the same companies as the tour operators. As one high-street consultant told me: 'You look at those brochures you get the commission on first, then look at others if they don't suit the customer.' So in some agencies you'd be encouraged to sell products that will make more money for the agency, rather than those that are necessarily the best for the customer. Rosalind agrees that this happens: 'I'm absolutely certain others do. They're looking at the short-term bottom line. But largely the public brings it on themselves because they say "I want the cheapest" – and you're not necessarily going to get what suits you. And at the end of the day, we're actually an agent for the tour operator.'

Rosalind sums it up: 'It's totally commission basis, so if you don't make sales the agency doesn't earn any money. The larger agencies definitely are sales-based. It's just a different way of looking at things and that's probably why I've got a different type of clientele.'

Travel consultants tend to have a low basic wage and earn the rest in incentives: 'It's not commission as such, but if they book something they get a certain amount per traveller,' says Jane. 'It's not based on the value of what they sell. Each different travel agency will negotiate with each different tour operator to incentivise for the members of staff.' The amount of salary compared to incentives varies with the different agencies, and this is something worth checking out. In smaller agencies, says Rosalind, although there's still a commission element, it's not so important: 'Here, we all have a target and if you achieve target then a bonus kicks in. If you don't achieve target then you get, within the industry, a reasonable amount.'

Hayley Williams of Holiday Hypermarkets enjoys the incentive aspect of the work: 'I wanted to go into a multiple agency, as they're more target-driven. I like that. I like getting recognition as top seller and so on. I did two years with a multiple and was promoted to assistant manager. It's fun and you do learn a lot if you work yourself way up: you can earn well with incentives.' Clarissa agrees: 'When it gets busy, like in January, we all get very high commission and when it's quieter there's less.'

Agency managers are always trying to increase the amount earned through commissions, and the services available through travel agencies are therefore increasing: travel insurance is now a major element, as is advance car hire.

PROMOTION PROSPECTS

There's a ladder to climb within agencies: you may start as the office junior but if you like the work and do well, you could rise to assistant manager, then manager and on to area or group manager over time. 'In smaller agency work, they usually say that you're not in the same place for more than two years,' says Hayley. 'If you stay at the same place for too long you can feel like part of the furniture. You want to move up the ladder, get promotion.' Smaller offices may not have the opportunities in-house, so you need to be prepared to move within your company or transfer to another company. Staff turnover does tend to be higher than in the past, and now it's possible to get promotion within a year.

An assistant manager helps the manager out and runs the office when the manager is away. The manager looks after the whole unit, including training and managing staff, recruitment, paying bills, handling complaints, and so on.

Meteoric rises are possible. This is Jane Barter speaking about her time in high-street agency work: 'We won the Top Shop in our area the first year after I became manager, in terms of sales, customer service, selling the right products, car hire and foreign exchange. It was determination. I'm really determined – I want to be the best at everything and I wanted to explain that to my staff: that if you work hard you reap the benefits. Then I went to a shop that was underperforming: I sorted the staff out there, then we started turning the business round in that shop and we won Top Shop. Then they asked me to go to one of the bigger shops in the area; again it was really short-staffed; it wasn't underperforming but it needed management.' But how does she do it? 'It was intuition – I had some management training, the odd day here and there, but I'd been so long in the business: you learn from mistakes, what works here and doesn't work there.

'You've got to have your staff behind you before they'll work for you. They've got to enjoy coming to work, so it's got to be fun. You've got to be there for them. If they're happy at work and enjoy what they do they're going to perform well for you. You can do anything in business as long as you can manage people.'

Jane now manages a Holiday Hypermarket and describes the opportunities: 'One of the **welcome crew** is interested in admin so when we're not busy I'm training her so she can move there later if she wants to. If a head of department leaves to another unit then there is room for promotion and to move along. You can move sideways and up.'

But is agency work a good start in the travel business: can you go into an agency then up and out? 'I have!' says Jane. 'You can move to a call centre, to one of the Internet companies: that's a big new thing; there's business house travel, corporate accounts. Then you can move to the airports. Most people who are in travel tend to stay in travel – once you've got it in your blood, you may move away for a couple of years but nine times out of ten you'll return. Once you've got your foot in the door of the travel industry there is so much you can do. Because you are dealing with customers you can move to reception in a hotel or other work within other service areas. It's definitely more of a career thing now than it used to be: there are so many opportunities now for me that I never thought would happen when I started in travel agency.

'You get what you want if you're determined. That applies to anything in life: if you want something that badly you'll do it.'

PERKS

As a travel agent you need to know about travel and destinations, but your work is office-based. So how do you find out? One way is to go on educationals. Tour operators want you to know all about their holidays – and how good they are – so that you will sell these holidays to your customers.

Clarissa Bowley has been on two educationals in her two years in travel: 'I went skiing in Andorra. That was really good. It was four days, two days spent actually skiing and then two days of hotel trips. You get to know the hotels, and they show you the night life as well. We had to work through a work pack with questions about the resort. The other educational was to Rotterdam, and we stayed in a village like Center Parcs with lots of sports facilities and a big swimming pool. That was just a couple of nights.'

Although these trips are indeed educational, they are often now used as incentives to persuade staff to sell more of the product, and may be offered to the person who sells the most package holidays in a certain month, or to the most successful agent in the region.

TRAINING

You can go into a travel agency after doing a college course, or straight from school. Either way, you may go in under a government training scheme called a National Traineeship or a Modern Apprenticeship (see Appendix 3) or as a regular trainee employed by the agency.

Clarissa Bowley chose the college option: 'I did my GCSEs then I left school and decided I wanted to go into travel – it really interested me and I thought I'd give it a try. I started with a one-year travel course full time at technical college. It included the ABTA [Association of British Travel Agents] exam, British Airways ticketing, computer skills, and an NVQ in travel. We were taught a lot about the products. We did presentations in groups about destinations. There was one day a week work experience: I worked in a flight specialist then I was transferred to a large high-street chain. I enjoyed that.'

Another travel agent describes her training in a high-street agency: 'It was mainly watching other people selling,

helping out with the brochures and getting to know products. Also there was an introductory course, a foreign exchange course and a systems course.'

Jane Barter gives a manager's view of the training young people get in agencies: 'We do need more travel agents and the high-street agents are good, they have got fantastic training schemes and they're giving new people a chance. There're not that many going off to college and doing the qualifications, so it's good to train in a placement and have hands-on experience.'

Hayley Williams doesn't see the need for a college course first: 'With travel agency, you can't just learn through a college. More young people who want to be in travel are now going to college to do travel and tourism courses, but they're not really geared towards agency work. I feel you learn more on the job. It's a good idea to do this but only if you don't know what you want to do in travel. I started as a YTS [the scheme that has been replaced by National Traineeships] in an independent travel agency. You start making the tea and then work up. I did two days a month in the college. I did three years at this independent agency and got NVQs level 2 and 3 in Travel Studies, also the COTAC 1 and 2, which was the old qualification before NVQs. After three years I was ready to move on.'

Jackie Brough started later in travel agency than most people – at age 34 after working as a care assistant. She went back to college to study for ABTAC, the ABTA travel agencies certificate. 'I was very keen to secure a job whilst still at college,' she says, 'so part way through the course I contacted West Midlands Co-op Travel. I was offered an interview for a couple of weeks' time. However, I was very persistent and said that I was available for interview that day and fortunately they agreed.' She started work on the foreign exchange counter and moved over to become a travel agent six months later. She continued with her college course part time and passed the exam with flying colours. A year later, Jackie came top in the Co-op Travel's staff incentive scheme, winning a car.

There should be on-going training once you have finished your college course and any initial training scheme. 'We are taught to sell,' says Clarissa, 'lots of tips on what some customers can come up with, and what you can say to encourage them to book. Sometimes we have quizzes here, and they encourage us to read the brochures and take them home.' Managers will walk around giving 'coaching', seeing how you're doing, and if you need any help. There are meetings to discuss how sales are going and to encourage you to think as a team and all work together towards agency targets. As you progress, you may choose to start new courses in ticketing, for instance, or foreign exchange, or perhaps to gain one of the travel NVQs. There is more on training and qualifications in Appendix 3.

INDUSTRY CHANGE

Retail travel is undergoing a shake-up. High streets are still full of travel agencies but more of these are linked in with the large holiday groups and there are fewer independent, locally run agencies.

As well as this, new technology is giving people new ways of buying their holidays. You can book a holiday via teletext or the TV Travel Shop. There are Internet companies with websites offering cut-price deals. All the tour operators and airlines run their own websites, or at least are thinking about it, as a way of selling their products direct to the public. Many already encourage holidaymakers to book directly with them by telephone, either after visiting their website or looking at their brochure (which they may have picked up at the local travel agency!).

And on top of all this, some suppliers are cutting or removing commission for the holidays or flights that agents sell, and replacing them in some cases with a flat fee. Some tour operators are placing their direct booking phone number prominently on each page of the brochures that they then send out to the travel agencies. Agents say they cannot continue selling these products if they don't get paid. Some are talking about charging the public a fee or a commission: then they would effectively be selling their services as advisers.

It's not just ownership and commission that are changing: it's also location. Some customers want an out-of-town agency where they can park easily, where there's entertainment for the children and a chance to talk to experienced consultants whose telephones never ring. Additionally, call centres are a huge and growing part of the travel industry (see the Call Centre Staff section).

A lot of this change is very exciting; some of it can be worrying, especially if you are thinking of joining a high-street travel agency. So what is going to happen next?

THE FUTURE

Rosalind Wolfarth, the independent travel agent, has some thoughts about what will happen in the future in travel retailing: 'The type of customer that books on teletext and uses the Internet will do without us anyway. But there will always be room for independent agencies. You cannot just switch on a machine and say: "I want all this information." You go into an agency and ask someone, and they have a computer in their brain that works overtime and knows where to go to get the information very quickly.

'I think you will see a lot of agents going out of business, and not necessarily the independents. Knowledgeable people in the agencies will be fewer and fewer until people can't get the information they want and then they'll be forced on to the Internet kicking and screaming, and then they won't get the service that we can deliver. There'll be a call for them eventually. People will say: "Well, I used to be able to go into the travel agent and they would give me really good advice," but unless the advice that goes out of the door comes back in and is rewarded, we can't deal with it.

'In this day and age about ninety per cent of people come in and say "I'm looking for a cheap ..." whatever.

It's quite disheartening; even a lot of the well heeled think they will do better doing their own research, and they won't necessarily.'

Jane Barter, Holiday Hypermarket manager, agrees with Rosalind about the future need for travel agents: 'I don't think the high-street travel agent will ever go. A lot of people do like to speak to someone; they like to have face-to-face contact. I think there's enough room for everyone.'

Whatever customers want, right through the industry there's a feeling that there will be a shake-up of travel agencies, but that there will always be a demand for them and the service they offer.

SKILLS YOU NEED

● To enjoy working with the public: 'You have to be confident and approach people and be chatty, get them to sit down' (Clarissa).
● 'You need to be able to have x number of balls up in the air at the same time. You need to be able to juggle your work: stop, start, stop, start. People don't last in travel if they're not prepared to be flexible. You need this ability to stop and start and not need to carry a job through at your own pace when you want to do it. If you aren't good at that you'll find it infuriating' (Rosalind).
● Teamwork skills, as well as being able to work independently.
● An interest in and some knowledge of geography.
● Computer literacy.
● Good basic English.
● Numeracy, as you're dealing with figures the whole time.

● Attention to detail.

● Sales skills, or the potential to gain them.

● Organisational skills.

● Common sense.

● Endless patience. 'You need to be able to bite your tongue at times. Sometimes you need to be quite a good psychologist' (Rosalind).

● You need to be enthusiastic and bubbly, not over the top but pleasant. You've got to be excited for the customer, even though you're not going on the holiday.

● It'll help if you have GCSEs in English, maths and geography, though these aren't essential.

● Languages: 'Generally there's not a huge call for languages though we have a good range of languages here' (Rosalind).

● Age: 'People with more experience of life are able to deal with customers in an understanding way; they are usually more confident and have the ability to listen to what the customer wants and respond accordingly' (Geoff Hurmson, West Midlands Co-op Travel).

PRACTICAL INSIDER INFORMATION ON HOW TO GET THE JOB

It's not as hard to get into travel agency work now as it was, says Jane Barter, because of the youth training schemes available. When you first start looking, you might need to do some legwork to find suitable places to apply. Hayley Williams explains how she started off: 'When I first started I went round all the travel agents and asked: "Can you help me?" They advised me and then I

went from there.' Other places to look for work include the local press, the careers centre and your careers teacher (for details of training schemes), and the head offices of large chains of agencies. Also try the Travel Training Company (see address below). If you are at college, employers may contact the staff looking for suitable trainees, so ask your tutors.

You need a CV that shows you have the qualities listed above, and that you are very keen to work in travel. Make this clear in the letter you send with your CV, if you are sending it around to agencies on spec. Some employers will ask you to fill in their application form, in which case you can use some of the information from your CV to answer the specific questions on the form. Don't send the CV as well.

Most interviews will be one-to-one, though it's possible that a larger organisation might arrange group interviews first: if you're not told what the process involves, call to ask. Jane recruits for Holiday Hypermarket. She looks for 'people actually asking me questions, not just me doing all the questioning. It shows that they're interested, that they can actually ask lead questions, which is what they're going to have to do when they're with a customer. It's really important that they're going to get on with the rest of the team: there are lots of things I look for but it's also a feeling I get. Sometimes the shy ones, after a bit of developing and coaching, can be really good sellers. It's just confidence.'

Jane describes one candidate who came to her for a job when she was recruiting for a high-street travel agency: 'She was working in a pub. She had won awards for customer service in the pub and hadn't really travelled a lot and had no travel industry experience, but she had a fantastic personality. She could really hold a conversation; she was amusing, and she was keen to get into sales. I took a chance on her, and she turned out to be a top salesperson.' Above all, Jane says: 'I look for people who are confident and who really want the job.'

GLOSSARY

● **Closing the sale**
The part of the selling process when you ask the customer to buy. It might not be obvious: you might gradually work through all the aspects of the holiday until the customer comes to accept that they do want it.

● **Educationals**
Free or subsidised short visits to resorts to enable you to tell the clients back home all about it.

● **Retail**
An industry term meaning the travel agency side of things.

● **Welcome crew**
These are people in larger agencies (and other retail outlets) whose job is to welcome customers into the shop and direct them to the right area or help with general queries. In smaller agencies, all the staff would be on the lookout for 'lost-looking' customers and would welcome them into the shop.

USEFUL ADDRESSES

The Travel Training Company might be able to arrange a National Traineeship (NT) or Modern Apprenticeship (MA – see Appendix 3) training placement for you. Call or write to them at:

● The Travel Training Company, The Cornerstone, The Broadway, Woking, Surrey
GU21 5AR. Tel: 01483 727321.
ttp@tttc.co.uk; www.tttc.co.uk

TRAVEL WRITER

We all need to know what it's like 'out there', but most of us don't have the time or money to travel as much as we want, so we read about other people's experiences in travel books, reserve the hotels they recommend in their guidebooks, and buy the products they promote through their brochures.

There are different sorts of travel writers: this section is about the ones who work in the travel biz by writing features and guidebooks rather than those who trek around the world then write a book about their experiences. Many – perhaps most – travel writers work part time at writing and mix it in with other things. This may be another type of work altogether, another type of writing or, of course, travelling. It's a good way to finance your travel, if you get the formula right.

GUIDEBOOKS

Your local bookshop has scores of books covering every tourist destination in as many different styles as there are types of traveller. These guides give a flavour of an area or country to be visited, as well as practical advice on what to wear, how to behave and which beaches are best avoided. Richard Trillo works for Rough Guides, a specialist publisher of guidebooks. He is now their Marketing, Publicity & Rights Director and stills writes freelance for them, as well as doing occasional travel journalism. His background experience for this was 'all on the job, apart from a couple of years at a travel agency selling Africa'. He says this about the work: 'As a budding travel writer you should focus on one or two broad destinations (like Africa, or South America, or Italy) and make them your personal expert subject. It also helps to have other areas of expertise that cut across, like motorbiking, or food, or ornithology.

Spending a good length of time in a place – not just a month here and a month there, but really getting to know Egypt for a year, or spending a year teaching in Sri Lanka or something – always pays dividends, and gives you a big morale-boosting cushion to collapse on to when things aren't working out financially.' He offers this warning, though: 'Nothing is ever as glossily painted as it appears from a distance. Close up it's full of cracks, flaws and detail. More interesting, less thrilling.'

Andrew Farr is a good example of a travel industry person who is also a part-time writer. He had a full-time job as a transfer representative in resort when he wrote his books under the pseudonym Dexter T. Haven: 'I wrote two guidebooks on Tunisia, and I've sold six thousand copies of one. I had a bit of a captive audience: I used to do my transfer speech, which was far too anecdotal and comic. I used to say to people: if you've enjoyed listening to that for an hour, buy the book.'

Andrew didn't write to make money, but rather to provide visitors with something that was missing from their holiday: 'I thought visitors to Tunisia could benefit. Up to that point, people weren't having the best holidays they could because they didn't have enough knowledge of how different the culture was.' For Andrew, it was important to have lived in the country and to have worked in the travel business. 'You need to know what people need to know on holiday,' he says.

He didn't want to get drawn into the UK publishing scene, so published the book himself in Tunisia: 'That way, I keep control of it,' he explains. And even though he is now UK-based, it's still selling: 'I came to an arrangement with the area manager, and she's managing it for me. It took me two years' worth of days off to write. It was fun to do, and it was a lovely moment when it came out: I'd been away for a few days and came back and there it was sitting on the coffee table at home. I've had some very nice comments and letters from people. It's still selling quite well.'

FEATURES

Writers such as Richard Trillo write occasional pieces of journalism in the form of features for a range of newspapers and magazines. Some travel writers specialise in this type of work. Jeremy is one. He spent a year doing a postgraduate course in Periodical Journalism and went from there. 'I started sending pieces off, and gradually built up a bit of a name,' he says. 'I do other types of journalism, too, because there isn't enough demand for pieces from someone like me, who isn't a constant traveller.' Jeremy usually writes up and sells pieces about his holiday trips. Others find enough of a market selling to periodicals while travelling to finance those travels. As Richard Trillo says: 'If you long to travel, just travel. Write and do things while you move. Travelling cheap is always cheaper than staying put.'

Being a photographer as well is an advantage. If you can supply great shots as well as great **copy** there are more markets open to you, though it's not essential: many editors are happy to use library shots.

BROCHURES

Holiday companies need brochures and these are often written by freelance copywriters, usually working through agencies. These are experienced, specialist writers who have files of information and draft copy about the commoner destinations. They may travel out to the destination to do more research or, if it is a short piece using standard material, may already have enough research on file.

MOVING ON

Some writers find their careers growing within the publishing world. Richard Trillo found himself a part of the Rough Guides organisation after writing a book for them and borrowing a desk in their offices to finish it. He is now in charge of 'the promotion and publicising of Rough Guides and nurturing and exploiting the brand'. He describes his job as comprising 'lots of e-mails. Lots of deadlines.' But he finds it varied and often rewarding, with plenty of travel opportunities. And there's still the thrill of seeing his name in print. 'The best bits are the publicity coups,' he says, 'along with the evidence that we're breaking into new markets. The less brilliant parts include the admin and the routine piles in the in-tray.'

SKILLS YOU'LL NEED

Richard says: 'I was always fixated about travel, from my earliest years,' and certainly you can't be a travel writer unless you love travelling. It can be gruelling work, involving a lot of detail, as well as working to deadlines and producing professional copy from the middle of the desert or the far side of the globe. Sometimes there's very little money in it. You've got to love the whole process, travel and all.

'Good typing is also a help,' says Richard. 'Good writing ability is essential to get into travel publishing on the writing or editorial side. Being very Internet aware is essential.'

PRACTICAL INSIDER INFORMATION ON HOW TO GET THE JOB

It's very competitive. Richard advises people to: 'Do what you enjoy. Be persistent. We often take people on as writers who have written exceptionally good letters to us after taking a Rough Guide and sending us their comments about it.'

Journalists usually train for a year following a degree. There are plenty of specialist books and courses on writing, writing markets and how to get your work up to standard and published.

GLOSSARY
● **Copy**
The material (words) you send to the editor.

VISITOR SERVICES MANAGER

TRAVEL RATING: 3/10. Sadly, the world comes to you, not the other way around. Essentially office-based, you'll go to travel trade fairs at home and abroad from time to time.

MONEY: Assistant level starts at about £13,000, perhaps less in the provinces. Officer level, the next one up, earns about £18,000. Manager: £20,000s to £30,000. Most attractions are owned by the state, local councils or charities like the National Trust, so generally salaries don't rise much above this. You might earn more if you work for a successful privately owned attraction like a theme park.

HOURS: Office hours plus some weekends and evenings, even occasional nights.

HEALTH RISK: 2/10. Most visitors are non-violent and most attractions are safe places to work. Ancient (and less ancient) monuments do occasionally burn down, but health and safety regulations should ensure you're out of the building at the time.

PRESSURE RATING: 4/10. Less pressured than a lot of travel and tourism work but there are constraints against reaching your financial targets that might stress you: for instance, if you work for a stately home you can't boost earnings by installing a bingo hall.

GLAMOUR RATING: 2–7/10. Depends where you work: meeting film stars and attending VIP banquets can be fun; you don't have to tell your friends you were there in a business suit organising the caterers.

*The UK has a huge incoming tourist trade: we attract culture vultures like Tudor queens to a chopping block. Visitors come from all around the world to go 'Gee' at our castles, 'Aaaah' at our countryside, even 'Ooooh' at the Millennium Dome. Every attraction of any size will have a person or team in charge of promoting their organisation. It's a **marketing** role targeted directly at visitors, or at the people who organise visitors' trips.*

Cara Bowen is Marketing and Visitor Services Manager at the Royal Pavilion, Brighton. This is a Regency palace and a major UK attraction receiving over 350,000 visitors each year. Part of her role involves marketing the Pavilion to organisations wanting to hold VIP banquets, to film companies looking for a location, to magazines such as *Vogue* needing a backdrop for their photographs, and to couples planning their wedding. 'One mother-of-the-bride had to come and measure the doorway before the wedding,' she says, 'to check that her hat would fit through.'

Cara spends the rest of her time attracting visitors to the Pavilion. 'Basically, it's cultural tourism,' she says. 'That means tapping into people whose main reason for travel is to have cultural experiences. It's a really big market, particularly in the UK. We have visitors from all over the UK as well as the USA and Europe, especially France, Holland and Belgium.' Cara must persuade these tourists to visit her site in preference to others.

There are many different aspects to this role, some of which she fulfilled when she first arrived at the Pavilion as their Promotions and Public Services Officer. 'That sounds like I cleaned the public toilets,' she says (and she is in fact responsible for these, and all visitor services). 'I'm in charge of all the facilities for visitors. I take an active role in making sure that the whole of the building looks good: I manage the franchise for the tea room, and when the toilets are refurbished I decide how they are going to look and push it through. I am also in charge of the signage around the building.'

She's also responsible for managing the staff in her division, including everyone **front-of-house** and the functions staff. She has a part in recruiting these staff, which last year meant ten posts, with approximately 75 interviews. 'We take on seasonal guides and cashiers, so recruitment is a big part of the job,' she explains.

She is also responsible for 'interpretation'. This is deciding how to present the building to visitors through the guidebooks, tours and so on. Cara makes sure the tour guides have any new research and information they need, and spends time listening to new guides to ensure they're saying the right thing.

Her visitor attraction work is a major part of what she does. 'I plan the advertising,' she says. 'I have an annual spend and have to research, buy **space** and write the **copy**, then get the graphic designers to do the layout and see it all through.' She advertises in historic house guides, British Tourist Authority publications and American, French and Belgian publications. 'I also plan and attend travel trade fairs, such as World Travel Market, held at Earls Court in London each November, and the British Travel Trade Fair at the NEC in Birmingham each March. I plan the graphics, literature, **press packs**, staffing and so on. Then I'll go and speak directly with people in the trade, perhaps meet phone contacts face to face. It's one of the key marketing areas, because we have direct contact with the trade.' By 'trade' Cara means the people who organise excursions to attractions such as the Pavilion. These could be tour operators, coach companies, excursion organisers for groups such as the Women's Institute, social club groups, and teachers.

An important part of Cara's job is maintaining databases and mailing lists for **direct mail**, making sure that clients are sent details of prices, special offers and other promotional material, as well as arranging advertising and brochure distribution direct to customers.

Finally, she is in charge of the

market research necessary before any of these marketing strategies can be planned and implemented. 'This is on-going in the building, with visitors' questionnaires. These ask what nationality they are, what publicity they saw, and other questions, as well as asking for feedback on their visit. The cashiers also ask every visitor their nationality when they buy their ticket. This all informs your marketing spend. It's cheaper to attract more of the same sort of person than to attract the sort of people who aren't visiting at all. In tourism terms, it's getting people through the door that counts.' Cara also commissions research from outside organisations, which will interview visitors and set up **focus groups**.

THE GLAMOROUS BITS

Filming is an important part of the marketing work that goes on at the Pavilion, and it's in two main areas: filming that brings in money in location fees, and promotional programmes that will help boost visitor numbers.

Promotional filming is usually for programmes focusing on Brighton, such as an edition of *Wish You Were Here* or *The Holiday Programme*. For these, Cara manages the visit to the building and provides interviewees, sometimes being interviewed herself.

Using the Royal Pavilion as a film location is important: 'I have an income target to meet,' says Cara. 'We had a bumper year last year as they filmed *The End of the Affair* here, a major feature film. They filmed through the night for two nights, as we

don't close the Pavilion to visitors during the day. I was there for one of those nights. There were about a hundred crew, and the whole place was taken over.' Cara is responsible for making sure that no damage is done to the Pavilion while they're there. In the instance she mentions, although she was up all night she worked the days either side of it, too. 'That's one end of the market,' she says. 'At the other end are corporate training films, or something like the recent BBC Educational programme on the life of the Buddha. They filmed here for four hours to get some background scenes.' Is it glamorous? 'It's really boring. There's so much hanging around. The two nights they filmed *The End of the Affair* ended up as about three minutes of the finished film.'

SKILLS YOU'LL NEED
● A degree.
● At least one European language at good conversational level. You may need to proof-read in that language and write business letters.
● Excellent written and oral communication skills.
● Good presentation and public speaking skills for media interviews, familiarisation visits, etc.
● Marketing experience/qualification.

PRACTICAL INSIDER INFORMATION ON HOW TO GET THE JOB

You won't go straight into paid work in cultural tourism marketing. 'The way to get into the arts and museums is to do voluntary work. You can do postgraduate courses in subjects such as arts administration, and they help, but the key element is experience. I worked as a volunteer in an arts centre for a year. I also worked in a shop and did ushering work. There are often lots of bits of work to supplement your income in an arts organisation.' Cara's advice on getting voluntary work: 'Places are always short of funds and need volunteers. Write in with your CV, and be specific about the area you're interested in. I only take volunteers on if they're specifically interested in marketing.' You can do this work in the holidays and at weekends. You probably need to do voluntary work for at least six months before employers will consider you.

From there you need to make lots of applications to any posts you see advertised, though you may be lucky and find a vacancy by word of mouth or internal advertising in the organisation where you volunteer. You'll need to be able to work anywhere in the country to stand a realistic chance of getting your first paid role. Jobs are advertised in papers such as the *Guardian* on Mondays, and in an arts marketing magazine called *Arts & Business*. 'There's not really a set career structure,' says Cara, 'so it can seem a bit random, and hard to get a job.'

When Cara looks at applications for her department she applies strict equal opportunities criteria, and awards point scores to each candidate. So it's important that you read the application form very carefully, especially the job description and candidate specification. Describe how you fulfil these criteria: don't be shy about your achievements. 'The work involves quite a lot of writing,' continues Cara, 'so it's important that people spell correctly and that it's neatly presented.'

At interview she expects candidates to have done their research about the Pavilion and the work. 'I ask them about their experience, and how they would react in certain situations – with the press, for instance.'

Other organisations may have less formal procedures, but you still need to be able to sell yourself to get a job in marketing.

GLOSSARY
● **Copy**
The text of an advertisement.
● **Direct mail**
Promotional information sent out to people in the travel trade. This is instead of, or as well as, advertising: it has the same purpose but is more closely targeted. You probably receive direct mail encouraging you to buy computers or clothes, or other items depending on which companies' mailing lists you're on.
● **Focus groups**
Small groups of carefully selected customers, assembled usually by market research companies to find out the answers to specific questions. At the Pavilion, focus groups would probably consist of people from their main visitor profile, which is women in their mid-thirties to mid-fifties who come to Brighton for a bit of shopping and culture. The Pavilion is a must-see to this group.
● **Front-of-house**
Anyone whose job is dealing directly

with the public, such as cashiers, guides and security guards.

● **Market research**

Gathering information from the 'market', in this case the visitors to the attraction, to find out what they want from their visit and whether they are satisfied with what they find when they do visit.

● **Marketing**

The business process of 'selling' your product. For instance, if you were marketing a castle as an attraction, your aim would be to fill it with paying tourists, conference delegates, and so on. It covers everything from market research at the beginning, finding out what people actually want to buy, right through to the sales process itself.

● **Press packs**

Packs of information given out to newspaper and magazine journalists alerting them to the selling points of the attraction, any new developments, and so on: anything that might persuade them to write an article about it.

● **Space**

The slot in a publication where an advertisement will go.

Winter Sports

The winter sports market is huge and growing, and many skiers travel with tour operators that employ the usual crew of reps to look after them. Independent travellers use locally run facilities, often staffed by an international crew.

Working in a ski resort is a lifestyle thing. Obviously, you're going because you want to ski, but there's more to it than that. 'It's brilliant; it's amazing,' says Joe Lynch of Neilson, an activity tour operator. 'You're meeting interesting people and you're in such a beautiful part of the world. One of the great things about this sort of work is the camaraderie. You're working with a team of people with similar interests – there're all there for the skiing and the fun. They're working hard to get the chance to ski.'

There are many different jobs, though not many British people do the most obvious one: ski instructing. As Joe explains, 'There are all sorts of restrictions on people from other countries teaching and taking trade away from the overseas ski schools – particularly in France. Instructors need the very highest level of teacher qualification [at least BASI level 3 – see Useful Addresses below] that you can get, but it's a small section of the market. The majority of people who go out on ski seasons are not ski instructors.' The few who are usually work through the specialist tour operators.

But there are other opportunities to enjoy a season being paid to ski. One great job is ski guiding, or companioning. You're not instructing as you're not qualified to teach, but you work in one of the larger resorts as a guide, showing people where the good slopes are and where to ski to avoid the queues. You'll probably work chalet holidays, where there's a group that wants to ski together. It is getting harder to find such work these days because of restrictions on people taking trade away from the local people.

Another job is 'chalet girl', a maid who can in fact be male or female. You work in the ski chalets where large groups of family, friends or sometimes strangers share the catering and other facilities. There's one large kitchen looked after by the chalet girl or girls. This is a typical day's work described by one chalet girl: 'We would get up to make breakfast for the guests, serve, tidy up after breakfast, and prepare the evening meal. If things had gone well we'd have that finished by twelve o'clock and return to the chalet at four p.m. to serve afternoon tea and cakes and start preparing the evening meal. So we'd have four hours' skiing a day. The company provided all the gear and the ski pass. On transfer day or if you have to overhaul the chalet you don't get out skiing. Pretty much everyone gets one day off a week.'

As well as these jobs there's other work with the tour operators in resort, and to support the resort itself: handymen (or rather handy people), reps, chefs, waiting staff, hotel staff, cleaners, plongeurs (kitchen staff), and so on.

TIMING

Winter season staff start in early December, set up for two weeks and work up to April, with January and February being the busiest months. As it's seasonal work, many people work the summer season elsewhere. Some people take time away from their careers to work the ski season: 'This winter we've had two lawyers working for us in skiing,' says one recruiter. 'You get a lot of professionals who take time off their professions: we have doctors, teachers – qualified professionals who have managed to get three or four months away from work.'

SKILLS YOU'LL NEED

It's hard, concentrated, people-based work, so the qualities outlined throughout this book apply here too. (Look especially at the section on Holiday Representatives.) Many people use a technical skill such as cooking or waiting table. Instructors need the appropriate qualification.

PRACTICAL INSIDER INFORMATION ON HOW TO GET THE JOB

See the Instructor section for more information on working with a tour company. You'll need to apply by July or August.

As for finding work independently, although most British people go out with tour operators you can apply for work in the hotels and other service areas direct. You'll find vacancies in the national press or a paper called *Overseas Jobs Express* (ask at your reference library). JobCentres have European work sections: ask there. Surf the Web for agencies representing tour operators and European employers – see one starting point below.

USEFUL ADDRESSES
● The British Association of
Snowsport Instructors (BASI),
Aviemore, Inverness-shire, Scotland
PH22 1QU. Tel: 01479 861717.
basi@basi.org.uk
● Surfing
Try agencies such as
www.natives.co.uk

APPENDIX 1

THE STRUCTURE AND STATE OF THE TRAVEL BUSINESS (PLUS SOME GENERAL ADDRESSES)

'Travel's a massive area, huge. When I came back from repping I remember looking for the first time at the *Travel Trade Gazette* and *Travel Weekly* and thought, My God, I'm looking at the wrong newspapers. I didn't understand a word of it: who's that; who are they? Everybody's linked up with everybody else. And growing.'

This insider sums up what many people feel when they take their first look at the travel industry: travel is huge; travel is growing. In a few years there will be organisations and jobs no one's even thought about yet.

This appendix aims to help by:
1 Defining some organisation types.
2 Looking at recent change in the industry.
3 Looking ahead at the future of the industry.

1 Here are the main types of organisations we have at present:

● Tour operators. Companies that package transport, transfers and accommodation, and sometimes entertainment and other extras, so that the holidaymaker only has to buy one product, not several.
● Travel agents. Sell holidays and flights to holidaymakers. Also cruises, car hire, entertainment, other travel, other ancillaries and business travel. Business travel agents specialise in selling to the business market.
● Holiday groups. There are a few main companies that own most of the tour operators and travel agencies in the UK. They gobble up the independents, then in turn are being gobbled up by European holiday groups. Soon the Intergalactic Travel Company will gobble everything, and if we want to go on holiday it'll have to be through them, via Uranus.
● Regulators and other institutions. There are organisations such as ABTA (the Association of British Travel Agents) and ITT (the Institute of Travel and Tourism, the industry's professional body), plus lots of others, which regulate, instruct or advise travel insiders.
● Public organisations. Councils and other public bodies have agencies working within travel and tourism, such as regional tourist boards and tourist information offices.
● Suppliers. The organisations that supply the accommodation, transport and attractions. This is a massive area in terms of employment.

2 Change within this structure: the main points

HISTORY

Travel and tourism used to be for rich people doing the 'grand tour' of Europe, empire-builders, and traders of all descriptions. Then came the first package tours. Thomas Cook kicked off with an outing from Leicester to Loughborough in 1841. The modern package holiday started about fifty years ago when Horizon and Club Med both started to bring low-cost foreign travel to ordinary people. Since then, hundreds of millions of holidaymakers have bought package holidays, and each year adds many millions more. Not all travel is packaged. Millions more people travel independently each year, both for leisure and business. Providing the services these people need is a huge part of the business too, as is satisfying the demand for business travel as globalisation increases.

GOBBLING

Larger operators in the business have swallowed up many of the smaller ones, leaving only a handful of large holiday companies along with fewer, smaller independents. They have also bought up many small travel agencies and reorganised and rebranded these. Many people are surprised that this is happening, as it is felt (by some) to be anti-competitive and misleading to the public. At the same time, many leisure travel groups are buying aircraft and running their own airlines, buying into hotel groups and controlling more elements of the package holiday.

RETAILING

There's change in the retailing of travel products – that is, the way we, the customers, buy travel. It is moving away from the high-street travel agent towards booking direct. E-commerce has a huge impact here.

NEW TECHNOLOGY

The travel business is expanding and developing to meet changes in its markets while also using the new technology which allows people to travel so much more cheaply, and for that travel to be administered more efficiently. Large operators are squeezing the agencies by cutting their commission rates (which is how they are paid – the client does not pay for the services of a travel agent) and replacing them with a smaller rate or a flat fee. Agents say they cannot survive on that basis; the operators dare not say 'good', but this is what they mean, since they believe that people will now book their travel direct.

BUSINESS TRAVEL

This has become more organised and separate from leisure travel to a greater extent, with specialist agents handling the needs of business travel.

CUSTOMER EXPECTATIONS

● Holidaymakers expect more: we want better transport, better accommodation, better food and location, better staff in resort, better transfers, better everything.
● Travellers expect more from the new technology. We want to be able to pre-book seats, to book holidays through our TV, to avoid the Saturday queues in travel agencies, to shop when we want to shop, and still magically find the right holiday.
● We want this more cheaply than ever before. Fluctuations within the industry and inaccurate forecasting have at times resulted in overcapacity

and too many holidays unsold. We have become aware of the trend to cut prices to shift unsold stock, and now expect a discount. Ninety per cent of customers use the word 'cheap' when they enquire about a holiday, according to one travel agent. But we still want top quality and have learned to create a fuss when we don't get it.

● The general public now complains. This, along with increasing concerns about health and safety abroad and new accountability, has been the major change within the tour operators' world.

3 The future

Here are some thoughts about the future, as voiced by travel insiders featured in this book:

● Competition for the inadequate supply of good-quality accommodation, especially competition with the emerging eastern European markets, is worrying the UK operators and causing them to buy up more hotels. We in the UK pay less for the same holiday than others in Europe (our contractors pay less for the same accommodation) and there is concern that we will be unable to compete for available beds.

● Will we all buy our holidays and travel direct, or will there always be room for travel agents? Perhaps we will adopt a model where we buy our standard seats and beds direct but sometimes ask a travel consultant for specialist advice on new destinations.

● Travel agents have traditionally been paid by commission; travel booked through an agent nets the operator typically 10 per cent less than travel booked direct. When operators stop paying agents their commission, will the public be prepared to pay a fee on top of the cost of travel? But perhaps it won't come to that: maybe there is a limit to the number of people prepared to book their own holidays direct, and the operators will pull back and accept that there is an on-going role for agents which they will need to fund through a commission or fee structure.

● We insist on 24-hour everything, so out-of-town holiday travel agencies are setting up which offer longer opening hours, parking, kids' play areas, themed activities, access to the Internet for direct bookings, and so on. Will these take over from the high-street travel agent?

● Call centres are a booming sector. We are used to tapping our requests into the phone, and waiting (and waiting). Will we become less tolerant of these, and the conditions of the workers there, or will they become more a way of life? Will there be enough people prepared to staff them?

● New technology is allowing operators to offer more sophisticated service and faster communication. This is a growing area of the business and will continue to be so, but to what extent will we tolerate the inevitable computer glitches?

● New destinations are emerging all the time; people want more and more and expect the operators to provide it.

Where will this end? And what will it do to our planet? (Look at websites such as www.ecotourism.org.)

THINGS THAT REMAIN THE SAME

● There are still plenty of jobs in travel: people are crying out for keen young people, though there's lots of competition for the work. You'll have to show that you're good and committed.

● You'll still have a wild time and see the world, if you get it right (the right job for the right person).

● You'll still be underpaid (initially at least) and still wonder whether cleaning was part of your contract of employment as you plunge the brush down the toilet.

● The glamour rating stays the same: the travel industry has never been glamorous/has always been glamorous – that depends on you.

● It's still a young industry, where you look twice at anyone over 45 – even over 30.

● It's also a fast-moving, exciting industry based around making people happy. 'If you're involved in an environment like that it has to rub off on you,' says an insider.

● It's still female-dominated numbers-wise (perhaps because starting salaries are too low for the more ambitious males of the species) and a good place for women to make a mark, though industry leaders are still almost all men.

GENERAL ADDRESSES

● Association of British Travel Agents (ABTA), 55–57 Newman Street,

London W1P 4AH. Tel: 020 7637 2444. www.abtanet.com; information@abta.co.uk

Go on-line for a list of all their members (650 tour operators plus over 7,000 travel agencies). Or contact ABTA for specific shorter listings, e.g. all the tour operators with programmes to Canada. ABTA cannot send out the full listing.

● Association of Independent Tour Operators (AITO), 133a St Margaret's Road, Twickenham TW1 1RG. Tel: 020 8607 9080. www.aito.co.uk; aito@martex.co.uk

The members are tour operators not owned by a larger organisation; they tend to be smaller niche operators. Some are also members of ABTA but you will get new contacts here.

● Institute of Travel and Tourism (ITT), 113 Victoria Street, St Albans, Hertfordshire AL1 3TJ. Tel: 01727 854395. www.itt.co.uk; itt@dial.pipex.com

This is the professional body of the travel industry. They send out a careers leaflet which may be useful.

LOCAL TOURIST BOARDS

● Scottish Tourist Board, 23 Ravelston Terrace, Edinburgh EH4 3TP. Tel: 0131 332 2433.

● Wales Tourist Board, Brunel House, 2 Fitzalan Road, Cardiff CF24 OUY. Tel: 01222 499909.

● Isle of Man Tourist Board, Tourist Information Centre, Sea Terminal

Building, Douglas, Isle of Man IM1 2RG. Tel: 01624 686766.

● Northern Ireland Tourist Office, St Annes Court, 59 North Street, Belfast BT1 1NB. Tel: 01232 231221.

● Cumbria Tourist Board, Ashleigh, Holly Road, Windermere, Cumbria LA23 2AQ. Tel: 015394 44444.

● East of England Tourist Board, Toppesfield Hall, Hadleigh, Suffolk IP7 5DN. Tel: 01473 822922.

● Heart of England Tourist Board, Woodside, Larkhill Road, Worcester WR5 2EZ. Tel: 01905 761100.

● Northumbria Tourist Board, Aykley Heads, Durham DH1 5UX. Tel: 0191 375 3000.

● North West Tourist Board, Swan House, Swan Meadow Road, Wigan Pier, Wigan, Lancashire WN3 5BB. Tel: 01942 821222.

● South East England Tourist Board, The Old Brew House, Warwick Park, Tunbridge Wells, Kent TN2 5TU. Tel: 01892 540766.

● Southern Tourist Board, 40 Chamberlayne Road, Eastleigh, Hampshire SO5 5JH. Tel: 02380 620006.

● West Country Tourist Board, Woodwater Park, Exeter, Devon EX2 5WT. Tel: 01392 425426.

● Yorkshire Tourist Board, 312 Tadcaster Road, York YO2 2HF. Tel: 01904 707961.

THE TRADE PRESS AND HOW TO GET IT

The two main general trade weeklies are the *Travel Trade Gazette* (TTG) and *Travel Weekly* (TW). There are also specialist papers within the different areas of travel.

TTG and TW are circulated free to people in the business, but others will have to pay for personal copies. Try to get hold of some hand-me-downs from people you know in travel, or befriend your local travel agent and ask for old copies. If you want to subscribe, call the numbers inside the papers concerned. Example rate: 50 copies of TTG (a one-year subscription) cost £98 delivered first class. There is a 50 per cent student discount but you need a tutor signature.

Your reference library may stock these.

APPENDIX 2

CAREERS AND FINDING WORK

Travel is such a fluid, fast-changing environment that you can plan to move in one direction and, a year later, find yourself doing something else entirely. That's not to say that you needn't reach for the stars, just that your route there might be more circuitous – and interesting – than you planned. There's no harm at all in planning, but insiders advise that it makes sense to be as flexible and ambitious as possible. As one travel veteran says: 'Years ago, a gap in the CV of people who had travelled was a problem. Now that the culture of the golden watch has gone it is acceptable for people to take a break in their mid-thirties, say. A CV that shows someone has stayed in the same job for ten years shows they are a plodder. People want achievers in the industry.'

So, what makes a good travel career? And how do you set about it? There are several recognised ways into travel, where the industry is geared up to taking beginners. These are listed below. You could split career beginnings into two main types, home and abroad:

● 'Start as a rep,' says a travel insider. 'You need to know what the guests are like. Last year I was working in the UK and overseas, and I saw how it fitted together. There are opportunities for a career in travel and the best place to start is overseas.'
● Other people start their careers in the UK, often with government training schemes within travel agencies and, to a lesser extent, other travel organisations. See Appendix 3 for more on government training schemes. There are other openings too: all the larger organisations (airlines, tour operators, and so on) operate some form of graduate or general training schemes.

A third option, remembering that the skills you need in travel are broadly similar to those of other customer service industries, is to start somewhere else in a customer service role, in retailing for instance, to develop relevant skills before moving into the travel industry. People sometimes make a career change by studying for one of the travel qualifications before they make applications. If you are at this stage, contact one of the specialist travel recruitment agencies for advice. These advertise in the back of the trade press (see the end of Appendix 1; also see Appendix 4).

The main bodies taking large numbers of people who are new to travel are:

● Tour companies looking for overseas staff. See the sections on:
– **Holiday representative**
– **Transfer representative**
– **Children's representative**
– **Administrator**
– **Tour manager**

● Various travel organisations looking for call centre staff.

● Travel agencies looking for sales consultants. (See the Travel Agent section.)

● Large numbers of people are also employed by airlines, airports and associated organisations, and cruise, ferry and train companies, but these people often have some travel industry experience. There are openings for people with other service industry experience here as well, though.

See:
- **Airline cabin crew**
- **Airline ground staff**
- **Airports**
- **Cruise staff**
- **Ferry cabin assistant**
- **Trains**

● Some people start in hospitality (hotels, bars, etc.). This is a sector in its own right, but see the Hotel Manager section for an introduction.

ON-GOING CAREERS

Overseas people generally start repping and progress from there. If you want to return to the UK and work in travel there are openings, but there's a lot of competition. 'Positions are minimal,' says a recruiter. 'A good company will offer an internal vacancy scheme where all vacancies within head office are advertised overseas. You have to be very determined and to know exactly what you want, and be the type of person to go into repping with the view that it's a career.'

Start with a travel agency and you'll find a more formalised career structure of assistant manager, manager, group manager, and on and up. You may also be able to move across to other areas of the travel business and back, as your skills will transfer easily.

You'll find structured career paths in some areas and organisations more than in others.

WHERE TO LOOK FOR WORK

Each section ends by describing the best way to start looking for work, with tips on how to get the job. Where there are no specific hints given, try these ways of finding vacancies:

● Writing on spec. Many travel positions are never advertised because so many people write speculative letters to the organisations they don't need to spend money promoting them. Write well-structured letters explaining what you want to do and why. Find out who to write to first by calling the organisation. There are helpful ideas about this at the end of the section on Sales and Marketing.

● Using the trade press. The two main general weeklies are listed at the end of Appendix 1, with information on how to obtain them. Each area of the industry has its own specialist press, but, because newcomers to travel won't be reading it, it's not the best place to look for ads. But it's worth scanning publications anyway, if you can, to get a 'feel' for what's happening. They're a good source of information for speculative letters.

● Using the national press. At certain times of year (see, for instance, the sections on Winter Sports and Holiday Representative) some companies place ads in the national press.

● Recruitment agencies. Vacancies may come through your college careers service, the JobCentre or private agencies. Look also for specialist agencies such as those for cruise staff.

● The Internet. Probably the best place to start some informal research. You may even find recruiters inviting on-line applications.

● Specialist books. Look at the listings of the best places to find specific work, such as support staff in ski resorts, or cruise staff, in the back of specialist books on these and other areas of the travel industry.

● Networking. Word of mouth is invaluable. Who do you know in the travel industry? Who might you know, if you started chatting to people around you about your ambitions? These people can often find openings that might not otherwise come to light. Talk to strangers in travel agencies and other travel organisations, too.

CAREERS ADVICE FROM INSIDERS

● 'Go for lots of interviews: it's the only way you're going to be confident. Whatever interview you go for you're going to be a bit nervous but go and talk to them, say you're willing to do anything, get used to interviews. I wrote a letter and CV, personalised them and sent them to twenty-five travel agents. People got back to me and I had interviews. I said I'd like to do something like a government training scheme. I got a job as a trainee. Go to the careers office to find out about the schemes on offer then do what I did and find a job that way.'

● 'Make sure you know why you want a career in travel. If it's because you want the easy and glamorous life you probably won't have it for long before you realise it's hard work, but it's great fun if you know what you're going in for.'

● 'Unfortunately the industry isn't moving towards having a graduate intake although all the bigger companies do have graduate training schemes. Youngsters tend to come in as school leavers at seventeen/eighteen; college leavers or people from other industries want to come into travel in their early twenties.'

● 'At the end of the day the success of any business in any industry will be dependent on the skills of those who work in it, and very much on the skills of the senior management, so the better calibre and quality of senior management we can have the better off we will be. If we can recruit a twenty-two-year-old who is very bright and has done a degree in travel and tourism and has a commercial brain by the time he's twenty-seven or twenty-eight, he's going to be making a good contribution to the success of our business.'

● 'If you're thinking of coming into the industry, ask yourself: Am I the sort of person who wants to get involved with a smaller company? Or do I want to get into what is in effect a corporate machine where I'm going to be working in an environment that is totally geared to delivering profit through innovative investment in our industry to make sure that they remain in a leading position? If you go down the smaller-company route you're going to get very much involved in all the aspects of the industry; you're probably going to learn a lot more much more quickly; you're probably not going to be paid as much as on the other side, but it could be a very good stepping stone for four or five years to a broader career in the travel industry. If you go down the corporate route you might get more formalised training; you'll certainly be at the leading edge or understand more about the leading edge of tour operation development, and it'll be very fast and probably quite exciting if you move up through the ranks.'

● 'We're aware that we will recruit people of a similar nature to us, and don't naturally go for stuffy people. Travel changes by the day. People from a regulated environment would go mad in a place like this.'

● 'People have to be outward-going, have a lively personality, not too shy, be quite proactive in their work, and want to come to work and go home at the end of the day feeling happy with themselves. It doesn't attract people who want a terribly regularised type of existence and want to know that they can have their coffee break at ten every day. It's a much more free-spirit type of environment and therefore people who succeed in it

and enjoy it will be that sort of person.'

● 'You've got to have keyboard ability, it helps a lot to have PC skills. You need to have a good telephone manner as wherever you work you'll be dealing on the telephone with clients or agents; being numerate is good; those are probably the basic skills just to get you into the industry.'

So: decide what you want, research it, work hard at applications, then be yourself, because travel people are interested in you for who you are.

APPENDIX 3

QUALIFICATIONS IN THE TRAVEL BUSINESS

Here's an outline of the qualifications you might be interested in, in two parts:

1 Those obtainable within education.
2 Those obtainable once you're in work.

You need to find out about these before you make any decisions: contact the relevant organisations for up-to-date information, and speak to your school, college and/or Careers Service teacher or adviser.

QUALIFICATIONS YOU CAN STUDY FOR WITHIN EDUCATION

These are relevant to you if you are still at school or at college full or part time, and probably not working, or not working within the travel business – in other words these are not training qualifications.

FURTHER EDUCATION LEVEL

These are courses that you normally take between the ages of sixteen and eighteen, the equivalent of A level study.

● You can take the usual A and AS levels, any additional GCSEs, etc., and progress into work or a degree course using this 'academic' route.
● You can opt for the 'vocational' route. This means courses that teach you about a particular type of work. The usual qualification is a GNVQ (General National Vocational Qualification). For the travel industry, the most relevant GNVQ is in Leisure & Tourism, and it's available at foundation, intermediate and advanced levels.

HIGHER EDUCATION LEVEL

This means university level.

● You usually study for a degree, though HNDs (Higher National Diplomas) are still available. HNDs are generally two-year courses. You may be able to lengthen these by a year to gain a degree.
● If you are interested in a vocational degree or HND (one geared towards a certain type of work), you may find that these are offered as 'sandwich' courses. This means that you spend a certain amount of your time working in the relevant industry in addition to your academic study. So sandwich degrees are often four-year courses, to include that time. These courses are structured in various ways, with differing periods of work experience.
● There are literally thousands of different degree courses. You may want a business course with a leisure or travel option, or may prefer accountancy or marketing, say, which, although they don't specifically prepare you for the industry, will help you progress in many jobs within travel if you're ambitious. Studying a language is an obvious advantage in the travel

industry. Course titles (taken at random) include:

- **Travel and Tourism Management**
- **International Travel and Tourism Management**
- **International Travel with Information Systems**
- **Sports and Coaching Studies/Transport and Travel**
- **Travel & Tourism Management with Italian**
- **Marketing Management/ Transport and Travel**

Go on-line to research these, or look at the Universities and Colleges Admission Service (UCAS) handbook (www.ucas.ac.uk).

QUALIFICATIONS YOU CAN STUDY FOR ONCE YOU ARE WORKING

These are workplace, or training, qualifications. A few people study for these before they find work in the hope that this will land them a job, but most begin them once they are in travel-related work. In some cases you will be doing them through your employer, who may pay for the training, run the course or give paid study leave. Alternatively you can do them in the evenings or weekends at colleges or through distance learning (what used to be called a correspondence course) and pay for them yourself. Here are the basic types of travel qualification, with a few examples of each.

NATIONAL TRAINEESHIPS (NTS) AND MODERN APPRENTICESHIPS (MAS)

These are national training programmes for young people (aged 16–24 when you start). They operate in many different industries. The travel industry schemes are run by colleges and other organisations such as the Travel Training Company. They are 'awarded' by organisations such as City and Guilds and the Royal Society of Arts. It is all very confusing! If you want to get an overview, contact the QCA (Qualifications and Curriculum Authority) or the SQA (Scottish Qualifications Authority). They will happily answer your questions or send you a free summary. At the end of your NT or MA scheme, you will, hopefully, achieve NVQs (National Vocational Qualifications) in travel subjects at levels 2 or 3. Your employer might keep you on as a regular employee.

Travel employers who want young people to work for them will often take them initially on these NT and MA schemes. It's the standard way into some areas of the travel business at this age. You aren't paid a wage but an 'allowance', which is at a government-set rate. The allowance is fairly low (a minimum of £75 a week in 2000, reviewed after six months – more for MAs as the entry requirements are higher). You might also get help with your travel expenses.

You will get on-the-job training as well as college study or distance learning packs.

You can find out about NTs and MAs via your school or careers office, your local TEC (Training and Enterprise Council), and the colleges and organisations that offer them. You might find that when you apply for an advertised job it is in fact for an NT or MA place.

NVQS AND SVQS (SCOTTISH VOCATIONAL QUALIFICATIONS)

Many people gain National Vocational Qualifications in their normal line of travel work, and continue to do so as they progress through their careers. They are awarded in areas such as Travel Services, Tour Operating, Leisure and Business Travel, or Guiding and Tour Managing, and so on.

The idea is that everyone who trains in work can get to certain standards, and these standards are graded. For instance, if you go straight into work after GCSEs, and train for a while, you might achieve an NVQ in Travel Services at level 2 or 3, say. NVQs aren't supposed to be 'compared' to educational qualifications (because they are a completely different thing – they measure your ability to do the work), but if we did, sneakily, look at them together we could say that they compare like this:

Academic level	NVQ level
● Some lower-level GCSEs	1
● Five good GCSEs	2
● A levels	3
● Degree or HND	4
● Postgraduate degree or professional qualification	5

Government training people are hoping that soon every skill you gain in the workplace will be given an NVQ level. This has already happened with most travel qualifications. It's a useful way to work out the level of training being offered to you, so do ask when you are researching training courses or thinking about doing work that offers training.

NB: NVQs are not GNVQs – they are completely separate. See the section on education above.

Both GNVQs and NVQs are organised by the QCA (Qualifications and Curriculum Authority) – see Useful Addresses.

OTHER TRAVEL QUALIFICATIONS

There are certain qualifications developed by and recognised within the travel industry, such as:

● International Air Transport Association (IATA) approved ticketing courses, for people who want to know more about air fares and ticketing, run in association with airlines such as British Airways or Lufthansa. You can qualify at two different levels. Many people in travel agencies need this qualification, as do others in the trade. It also carries NVQ ratings (showing how most qualifications now 'fit' into the NVQ system). You can gain this qualification at NVQ levels 2 or 3.

● Other courses/qualifications include the Association of British Travel Agents (ABTA) Travel Agents Certificate, the ABTA Tour Operators Certificate, and many others.

Your employer may help you with course and exam fees, or you may have to pay for these yourself. You'll find out more about these training courses and the qualifications you need as you progress.

Some organisations are great at training, others less so. The main point of this section is to emphasise that training in work matters: if you don't get it, you won't progress. Whenever you are looking at training and employment opportunities, ask – and research as much as you can about what the training involves, what you need to put in, and what you get out if it.

USEFUL ADDRESSES

● The Institute of Travel and Tourism (ITT), 113 Victoria Street, St Albans, Hertfordshire AL1 3TJ. Tel: 01727 854395. Itt@dial.pipex.com; www.itt.co.uk

This is the professional body for the travel industry. It deals with all aspects of the business and has a careers pack it sends to interested people. It registers and approves courses within higher education, doing more work at this 'management' end of the business than at school-leaver level. For information about careers and training at this earlier entry level, contact the Travel Training Company (see below).

● Qualifications and Curriculum Authority (QCA), QCA Customer Services, 29 Bolton Street, London W1Y 7PD. Tel: 020 7509 5556. Publications:

QCA Publications, PO Box 99, Sudbury, Suffolk CO10 6SN. Tel: 01787 884444.
GNVQ or NVQ enquiries:
Tel: 020 7509 5556
● QCA Northern Ireland, 2nd Floor, Glendinning House, 6 Murray Street, Belfast BT1 6DN. Tel: 02890 330706.
● Scottish Qualifications Authority (SQA), Hanover House, 24 Douglas Street, Glasgow G2 7NQ. Tel: 0141 248 7900.
● The Travel Training Company (TTC), The Cornerstone, The Broadway, Woking, Surrey GU21 5AR. Tel: 01483 727321. ttp@ttc.co.uk; www.tttc.co.uk

This is part of ABTA and is a training provider for the travel industry, mostly within travel agencies, though there is also a tour operator's certificate. But they will point anyone who wants to work in travel in the right direction, advising who to contact and sending out information. They help in placing NTs and MAs.
● Universities and Colleges Admissions Service (UCAS), Rosehill, New Barn Lane, Jessop Avenue, Cheltenham, Gloucestershire GL52 3LZ. Tel: 01242 222444. www.ucas.com

APPENDIX 4

WEBSITE ADDRESSES

As with all websites, details change and develop. Use these as starting points and follow links.

1 Recruitment agencies in travel – a few taken at random from the trade press:

www.aaappointments.co.uk
www.ukairportjobs.co.uk
www.candm.co.uk
www.maxwellrecruitment.ie
www.metrorecruitment.co.uk
www.newfrontiers.co.uk
www.bluestrawberry.com
www.townandcountry.ltd.uk
www.travelworldselection.co.uk

more senior positions:

www.harpwallen.co.uk

2 Go to the websites of any of the tour operators, transport providers or travel agencies and hop around; see what you can find. Their URLs are usually obvious but use the ABTA website or a search engine to track them down if you need to.

3 Just for fun: insider sites to sneak a look at. There are plenty more if you search around:

www.travel-library.co.uk
'a specialist stock photo agency covering a wide range of destinations, people and lifestyles'

www.seaview.co.uk
'a service that brings you news and information about the passenger ships that travel the great oceans and waterways of the world'

www.cruiseservicecenter.com/main.html
an insider's view of management solutions for cruises . . . some recruitment too

www.hsss.com/
'HSSS is a UK-based company providing a wide range of technology-based services to the European Hotel Industry'

www.ttctraining.co.uk/
'provides and develops training courses for the travel industry and produces and manages examinations for the major travel industry qualifications'

www.stlon.com/
supplier of travel and touring services to the music industry as well as corporate travel and conference and meeting organisation

www.coach-hire.uk.com
promoting the coaching industry

www.hometravelagency.com/dictionary/
Travel Industry Dictionary 'Searchable and helpful lexicon relevant to those in the travel industry'

www.itsnet.co.uk/in/home.htm
'Brings the "Information Super
highway" to the UK Travel Industry'

www.rail.co.uk/
UK railways on the Net

4 Remember to use the websites
listed in the main part of the book
too.